BLACK LIES MATTER

WHITE LIES TOO

"The most dangerous place for a Black man to
live, is in a scared, White person's imagination."
D.L. Hugley-

Jean-Baptiste Guillory

This book, like them all, I am forced to write under duress. It seems that there is a concerted effort, in some places, to reconstruct the history of so called Blacks and Whites. There seems to be a constant, full court press, to keep the racial divide going, to keep people up in arms and to keep people acting upon a substandard, if not entirely fake, historical education. It appears to be a certain core group of "academics," NOT ALL, who are hell bent on manufacturing and or creating this false historical narrative. Not only does it seem that they want to create this falsehood, but they want Black people, and Whites, to just accept this narrative without regard for whether or not it's true, or whether or not it matches the historical record, or whether or not it matches a family's genealogy. People are expected to just accept the narrative, and then go on to pattern their entire existence around that narrative, physically, emotionally, spiritually, mentally and most importantly, economically. People are expected to just capitulate intellectually because the "academics" say so, never mind if the "narrative" does not comport with reality. People have become so pliable on a mental level, so much so, that they will go entirely against logic and common sense, just because someone whom they feel is smart says so. So what is smart? Who are these "smart" people and how do they know whats best for everyone? First of all, the people who we look up to as smart, they "earned" their bona fidis from the same group of academics, club, or fraternity who cookie cutter out these aforementioned silly narratives. They call themselves, "Peers." That's where the term "peer pressure" came from. These smart academics take marching orders from the accounting office. (Remember, it's these "Peers" whose education has produced the current racial divide, for generations) Whatever party line is dictated, that's what the "Peers" teach. If one tiny deviation from the script is detected, that academic loses funding, "peer review" and is labeled a quack. That's fact... So when the word comes down, that all Blacks in America descended from "African" slaves, that all Whites were slave owners, inter alia, that no Black people fought willingly for the Confederacy, or Blacks didn't own slaves, including Whites, then that is what the teaching must reflect.

This book will present an alternative viewpoint of these issues. It is my own opinion, my own presentation. I am not an academic or affiliated with any. This author is not seeking, "Peer Review," as the opinion, critique or comments of others is meaningless to be honest, as this work is for "those who it is for," mainly my family. I will present the facts and let the reader make their own determination. I want to apologize up front because I'm probably going to insult you in some manner. If in fact you are prone to "micro-aggressions" or other similar silly ass foolishness, then this book "ain't for you," adios. Go get a comic book or some other meaningless distraction. This book contains adult, gritty, grimy language, adult topics, racial slurs, honest talk and hope for a change in perspective. As with all of these writings, it is my hope to open a different chapter in the way people view and treat each other. The fabric of an entire nation is being split, and the split is driven entirely by the total disconnect people have to their true historical past and how that past affects today's thoughts, intentions and actions in a negative way, thus perpetuating a cycle of evil, stagnation, low GDP and ignorance. People are a mess. In my previous books, "Ancestry Lost," and "Ancestry's Shame," I explained the meanings of certain words, and how those words blur the identity of so called Black and so called White people.

Presented in those books are perspicuous evidence of just how deep, obsessive compulsive, and fixated this nation has been on the issue of race. Literally "trillions" in GDP....flushed down the toilet while the "dogs chase their tails." Most readers would naturally assume this work would be focused initially upon Black people, however, White people are the ones who need the most work. Most people in the "world" take it for common knowledge that Black people have been fucked over in a vicious way, historically. There is no need to rehash each catastrophe, but for the sake of argument, we all except the fact that Black people have been fodder, and the recipient of the brunt of abuse. What most white people don't understand, because they are so completely brainwashed, is that while the Black people were getting their asses thrashed on a regular, the people who controlled the thrashing hadn't forgot about them. (Whites)

They had a different angle for the Whites. Give the Whites another entirely false, bullshit history, brainwash them into not only believing the bullshit "Africa/Slave" fairy tale, but to also "act upon" that tale in every aspect of their existence. The Whites became "Slave Masters" by default, whether or not if it was true, and whether they liked it or not. So here we are, generations of bullshit, generations of lost intellectual product, generations of lost GDP, generations of oppression and "academics," NOT ALL, supposedly teaching, educating and instilling wholesome values. What? You can tell a tree by the fruit it bears, and I just don't see it. Instead we have a divide in national unity, poverty, bloodshed and trillions in student loan debt. That recipe cannot continue if fiscal responsibility is to be maintained, it's a train wreck, just sayin'.

Its time for the conversation to change so people, collectively, can prosper and benefit the national, state and local environments in real meaningful way. That will never happen as long as the current psychological, racial, class and economic dynamic "between" peoples remains. Its been a treadmill mentally, intellectually and emotionally for generations, time to get off... or not, you decide?

WHITE SLAVERY

Lets start with Slavery. White people were slaves too, and not in some far off land, right here in America. We have to shatter that myth. Yes, white people, you were chattel too. I would like to start with the following quotes for context before we continue. There was a connection between Black and White people far more complex than modern history books espouse:

"It sometimes happens that the infant boy entertains a stronger affection for his Black nurse than for his white mother."
Kemble. F. Journal of a Residence on a Georgia Plantation, p. 194. 1864.

"Every Southern man in his memory runs back to the negro woman who nursed him; to the boy who hunted and fished with him; to the man who first taught him how to swim, and as he grew to manhood the cordial welcome given him by his nurse, with tenderness scarcely inferior to his mother."
Jefferson Davis, President of the Confederacy, Sex and Race, J.A. Rodgers, Vol. II p. 199, 1942.

Jefferson Davis (supposed NIGGER HATING PRESIDENT OF THE CONFEDERACY) was speaking from his own heart, his own experiences and his own conclusions. He speaks equally about, the woman, the boy and the man. "Niggers" as academics would have us believe,the vile slave from Africa, and yet the "President" of the Confederacy saw fit to make such a statement. He could have said, 'Yeah they're cool people,"or "I like them," yet he went on to say, "with tenderness scarcely inferior to his mother." Huh? That's some affection I'd say. People have to chip away at the myths. Slavery must be understood in a different manner if people are to really get past it and move forward personally or nationally. People have to understand that slavery was like crack in the 80s in L.A. Everyone had their hand in some aspect or another of its dealing. Either a person owned a store that sold drug paraphernalia, or a liquor store, or the police arresting people, or whatever. Everyone made some money off of the trade, and that's how slavery was. It was the crack of the ages, and only the invention of functional, practical steam and combustion engines changed that. If you lived in America you would be snatched up and sent any number of places, including Africa. If you were White on the other side of the world then the Moors were snatching you up and selling you. They (Moors) were even bringing folks here to America as slaves, as well as the Europeans. Many 'a chump got "knocked out" and shipped out of Europe to America.....White People!

"Rev J. H. Aughey said he was struck by the whiteness of some of the "Negros"...There is a girl who does not look very white in the face due to exposure but when I strip her to whip her, I find she has skin as fair as my wife." J.A. Rodgers, id p. 205
American Slavery As It Is, p.25 1839

"The Niles Register, June 9, 1821, "the people were out of their minds after seeing a woman and her children, "who were as white as any of our citizens, indeed, we scarcely ever saw a child with a fairer of clearer complexion than the younger one"... for sale at public auction amongst the Blacks."
J.A. Rodgers, id

"In August 1774, William Cunningham brought a number of Whites kidnapped in Ireland to America and sold them. He confessed on his death bed in 1791."

"Race! Do not speak to us of race- we care nothing for breed or color. What we contend for is, that slavery whether black or white, is a normal, a proper institution in society. The blood of orators, generals, statesmen, even the President of the Republic runs in the veins of men who are bought and sold like horses and mules. Slavery, white or black, is right and necessary."
George Fitzhugh. Sociology for the South or The Failure of Free Society p. 225 1854

"But the imagery of white slavery was dangerously unstable in an economy that was changing as fast as that of the urban South in the 1850s. It was in 1857, after all, that George Fitzhugh finalized his own famous solution to the anomalous presence of a white working class in a society based upon black slavery: Enslave them all. And, indeed, even as prosperous slaveholders were spending thousands of dollars at a time to buy near-white slaves to work in their households, they were employing increasing numbers of whites (and those, like the Irish, who were in the process of becoming white) as wage laborers, tenant farmers, and domestic servants. New Orleans in the 1850s, as the Louisiana physician and racial theorist Samuel Cartwright described it, daily offered more concrete examples of "white slavery" than did distant strikes or living conditions. "Here in New Orleans," Cartwright wrote in De-Bow's Review, "the larger part of the drudgery-work requiring exposure to the sun, as rail-road making, street-paving, dray-driving, ditching, building, etc. is performed by white people . . . a class of persons who make Negroes of themselves in this hot climate." As Barbara Jeanne Fields has put it, class relations between white people in such southern cities as New Orleans were being "drawn into [racial] terms of reference, as a ray of light is deflected when it passes through a gravitational field." According to Cart-

wright, the Irish were not becoming white, they were, like the white workingmen with whom they shared their days, turning black."
Published on Historical Society of Pennsylvania,'White Slavery' in the ante-Bellum South and Civil War Era: A Little Known Phenomenon'

White people for some reason have been erased from the slave narrative. Whites, and not just from Ireland were routinely kidnapped and sold into slavery every-where. There are stories of white people being kid-napped, including children and dipped in black dye to make their skin dark, it was called "bootlegging." Try to wrap your head around that. Preferably a young girl, 13 and under, kidnapped from her family, molested, passed around like trash, dipped in some sort of dye, having beeswax put in her hair to make it curly, taken to a slave market, threatened to be silent, or drugged and sold like a animal. A white person in America, land of the free.

Richard Hildreth, a 1850 historian noted how easy whites could be kidnapped and made into negro slaves, "Just catch a stray Irish or German girl and sell her... and she turns a 'nigger' at once and makes just as good a slave..."
J.A. Rodgers, id. pp.210

"The Abbeville Banner of Alabama tells of James C. Wilson, white, who married a white woman, and later sold her and her children to a preacher named, Guilford, as slaves. Later he sold his wife's 15 year old brother too."
Anglo African Magazine, Vol 1 p. 336 1859.

"The Philadelphia (PA) Public Ledger, for December 27, 1860, reprinted an article from a Natchez, Mississippi newspaper, entitled, "Painting a White Girl to Make Her a Slave." It was stated how a man from Natchez was on a steamboat on its way to Greenville, Mississippi, when he noticed a young girl, "aged about nine or ten years," with black hair and "yellowish brown skin." He was told she belonged to a gentleman on board who was taking her to New Orleans to be sold for $160.00. Talking to the young girl alone, the inquisitive passenger was informed by the girl, how " she was an orphan, and had been taken from an asylum in New York," and that her hair had been light originally, but her 'master' had a barber dye her hair black, and also put "some yellow dye on her skin." Soon after the above confession, the young girl was taken by the ship captain, who after using potash, soap and water, removed "the dyes...and the light hair and light complexion were brought to light." The pretended "master was seized by the excited passengers," who caused him to be locked up in a state room until the boat should land. The young girl was eventually placed in an orphan asylum in New Orleans."

"Cincinnati (Ohio) Gazette(reprinted in the Philadelphia Daily Evening Bulletin), related that within the 78th Ohio Infantry Regiment, was a man who was taken, "as a runaway slave," into the Union lines in Tennessee. His features and skin color denoted "Anglo-Saxon" ancestry, while his eyes were also "blue, his lips thin, and his hair light." His former Tennessee master had admitted to Colonel Mortimer D. Leggett, "that there was not a drop of African blood in the veins of his slave," and that he had purchas- ed the man in Richmond, Kentucky years before, and that he'd been "sold into slavery, out of some charitable institution to which he had been committed as a vagrant."

The Lebanon (PA) Courier, for April 9, 1863, contains a remarkable tale of a white man held as a slave. The account states how a planter's daughter in Mississippi

was seduced, and to "hide her shame" after she became
pregnant, her female child was given to a slave woman,
along with a certain amount of money, in order to
"bring her up as her own." The child eventually became
the "mistress of the planter's son, who succeeded to
the estate. She had by him five children, and among
them the man...Charles Grayson. This was in Calhoun
County, Mississippi, three miles from Paris." Eventually Charles was sold to William Steen, and soon after he
learned of his true parentage. Running away, he was
"captured and treated with harshness. He was made to do
more work than any slave.--The object was to break him
down. He proved to be strong and able to bear all the
burdens put upon him."On December 17, 1862, the Third
Michigan Cavalry came into the area, and Grayson pro-
cured a horse and rode into their encampment. There he
was employed as a cook for one of the non-commissioned
officers, Theodore Reese, of Company 'F.' He wished to
move North, and was thus aided by Lt. Col. G. Rogers as
well as citizens of Jackson, Tennessee, who assisted
Grayson in carrying out his plan. Not long after he
took up residence in Cass County, Michigan, where by
1870 he was working as a farm laborer for a Peter
Scofield and his family of Cass County. Charles Grayson
was a 'slave' for seventeen of his twenty-three years,
but his "straight, light hair, fair blue eyes, a sandy
beard," revealed that he was indeed a Caucasian and not
of Black ancestry."
Published on Historical Society of Pennsylvania,'White
Slavery' in the ante-Bellum South and Civil War Era: A
Little Known Phenomenon'

"In January of 1857 Jane Morrison was sold in the slave
market in New Orleans. The man who bought her was James
White, a longtime New Orleans slave trader, who had recently sold his slave pen and bought land just up the
river from New Orleans, in Jefferson Parish, Louisiana.
Morrison, apparently, was to be one of his last specu-

lations as a trader or one of his first investments as a planter. Sometime shortly after her sale, however, Morrison ran away. By the time White saw her again, in October 1857, they were in a courtroom in Jefferson Parish where Morrison had filed suit against him. Before it was settled, that suit would be considered by three different juries, be put before the Louisiana Supreme Court twice, and leave a lasting record of the complicated politics of race and slavery in the South of the 1850s. The reason for the stir would have been obvious to anyone who saw Morrison sitting in court that day: the fifteen-year-old girl whom White claimed as his slave had blond hair and blue eyes. In her petition, Morrison asked that she be declared legally free and white and added a request that the court award her ten thousand dollars damages for the wrong that White had done her by holding her as a slave. She based her case on the claim that her real name was Alexina, not Jane, that she was from Arkansas, and that she had "been born free and of white parentage," or, as she put it in a later affidavit, "that she is of white blood and free and entitled to her freedom and that on view this is manifest."Essentially, Alexina Morrison claimed that she was white because she looked that way. By the time Morrison v. White went to trial, Alexina Morrison would claim that her whiteness made her free, but when Morrison and White first met, in the slave market, it might simply have made her more valuable. It is well known that slaveholders favored light-skinned women such as Morrison to serve in their houses and that those light-skinned women sold at a price premium. What is less often realized is that in the slave market apparent differences in skin tone were daily formalized into racial categories-the traders were not only marketing race but also making it. In the slave market, the whiteness that Alexina Morrison would eventually try to turn against her slavery was daily measured, packaged, and sold at a very high price. The alchemy by which skin tone and slavery were synthesized into race and profit happened so quickly that it has often gone unnoticed. When people such as Morrison were sold, they were generally advertised by the slave traders with a racial category. Ninety percent of the slaves sold in the New Orleans market were described on the Acts of Sale that transferred their ownership with a word describing their lineage in terms of an imagined blood quantum-such as "Negro," "Griffe," "Mulatto," or "Quadroon." Those words described pasts that were not visible in the slave pens by referring to parents and grandparents who had been left behind with old owners. In using them, however, the traders depended upon something that was visible in the pens, skin color. When buyers described their slave market choices they often made the same move from the visible to the biological. When, for example, they described slaves as "a griff colored boy," or "not black, nor Mulatto, but what I believe is usually called a griff color, that is a Brownish Black, or a bright Mulatto," buyers were seeing color, but they were looking for lineage. The words the buyers used-griffe, mulatto, quadroon-preserved a constantly shifting tension between the "blackness" favored by those who bought slaves to till their fields, harvest their crops, and renew their labor forces and the "whiteness" desired by those who went to the slave market in search of people to serve their meals, mend their clothes, and embody their fantasies. They sectioned the restless hybridity, the infinite variety of skin tone that was visible all over the South, into imagined degrees of black and white that, once measured, could be priced and sold. As Monique Guillory has suggested in her work on the New Orleans quadroon balls, the gaze of the consumer projected a fantasy of white masculinity onto the bodies of light-skinned women: the fantasy that other people existed to satisfy white men's desires. Though that fantasy was particularly associated with the notorious "fancy trade" to

New Orleans, the sale of light-skinned women for sex or companionship occurred all over the South. The word "fancy" has come down to us an adjective modifying the word "girl," a word that refers to appearances perhaps or manners or dress. But the word has another meaning; it designates a desire: he fancies...The slave market usage embarked from this second meaning: "fancy" was a transitive verb made noun, a slaveholder's desire made material in the shape of a woman like the one slave dealer Philip Thomas described seeing in Richmond: "13 years old, Bright Color, nearly a fancy for $1135." An age, a sex, a complexion, and a slaveholder's fantasy.

A longer description of Mildred Ann Jackson traced the same lines: "She was about thirty years old. Her color was that of a quadroon; very good figure, she was rather tall and slim. Her general appearance was very good. She wore false teeth and had a mole on her upper lip. Her hair was straight." Jackson's body was admired for its form, for its delicacy, and for its fetishized details. The slave dealer James Blakenly made the density of the traffic between phenotype and fantasy explicit when he described Mary Ellen Brooks: "A very pretty girl, a bright mulatto with long curly hair and fine features . . . Ellen Brooks was a fancy girl: whiteness means by that a young handsome girl of fourteen or fifteen with long curly hair." Solomon Northup (12 Years a Slave), a free black who had himself been kidnapped and sold in the New Orleans market, remembered slave dealer Theophilus Freeman's account of the price that light-skinned Emily would bring in New Orleans: "There were heaps and piles of money to be made for such an extra fancy piece as Emily would be. She was a beauty a picture a doll one of your regular bloods-none of your thick-lipped, bullet-headed, cotton pickers." Freeman made explicit what lay behind the descriptions; according to the ideology of slaveholders' racial economy, which associated blackness and physical

bulk with vitality, such bodies were useless for production. Light-skinned and slender, these women were
the embodied opposites of those sought as field hands;
their whiteness unfitted them for labor. For slave buyers, near-white enslaved women symbolized the luxury of
being able to pay for service, often sexual, that had
no material utility they were "fancies," projections of
the slaveholders' own imagined identities as white men
and slave masters. And so, at a very high price, whiteness was doubly sold in the slave market. In the first
instance the enslaved women's whiteness was packaged by
the traders and imagined into meaning by the buyers
into delicacy and modesty, inferiority and intelligence, beauty, bearing, and vulnerability. These descriptions of enslaved light skinned women, however,
were projections of slaveholders' dreamy interpreta-
tions of the meaning of their own skin color. Indeed,
in the second instance it was the buyers' own whiteness
that was being bought. The fantasies they projected
onto their slaves' bodies served them as public reflec-
tions of their own discernment: they were the arbiters
of bearing and beauty; their slaves were the showpieces
of their pretensions; their own whiteness was made apparent in the bodies of the people they bought. By buying ever-whiter slaves, the prosperous slaveholders of
the antebellum South bought themselves access to ever
more luminous fantasies of their own distinction. And
so slaveholders were willing to pay a lot of money for
the right kind of performance. The better the slaves'
performance, the greater the value produced out of the
synergetic whiteness of slave and slaveholder. Ironi-
cally, these slave market syntheses of whiteness and
slavery, these costly flirtations with hybridity, were
underwritten by slaveholders' ideology of absolute
racial difference. The saving abstraction "black blood"
held the power to distinguish nearly white women from
really white ones, to distinguish what was essentially
performance from what was the performance of essence-

slaveholders generally believed that "black blood," if present, would be apparent in the countenance, conversation, or carriage of the one who bore its taint.' When a performance of enslaved whiteness was too good, however, the combination of "white" appearance and behavior could overwhelm the intended distinction; a slave could become "too white to keep," likely to slip aboard a ship or hop onto a train and escape to freedom. A virtuoso performance of whiteness could breach the categories designed to contain and commodity hybridity; a slave could step over the color line and onto the other side. Perhaps the slave trader who sold Morrison to White was thinking of that type of performance when he remembered that she was "too white." And perhaps that is why James White had apparently curled the young woman's hair and dyed it black after he brought her home from the slave market. According to most versions of the southern social order, Alexina Morrison-whether as enslaved white or passing slave-was not supposed to exist at all. But the color coding, black slaves and white supremacy, that characterized most of the political debate over slavery was unreliable as a description of the institution's everyday life. First, there was racial mixture and sexual predation: throughout the history of American slavery it was not always easy to tell who was "black." 'I Second, there was manumission: just as racial mixture made it harder to tell who was "black," manumission made it harder to tell who was a slave. The ultimate expression of slaveholders' property right-the right to alienate their property however they pleased increasingly undermined the ability of slaveholders as a class to keep race and slavery coextensive.' Finally, there were the slave trade and interregional migration: the antebellum South was a rootless society. The broad transition from an upper South tobacco economy to a lower South cotton economy and the domestic slave trade, through which as many as two-thirds of a million people may have passed in the antebellum period, had removed hundreds of thousands of people such as Alexina Morrison from the communities in which their identities were rooted. Through acts as small as lying about their past in the slave market or as audacious as running away and claiming to be white, many of the enslaved people forcibly transported by the trade worked their deracination against their slavery. By 1857, when Alexina Morrison ran away and sued the slave trader, southern lawmakers already had at least two centuries' experience with the ambiguities of a social order in which not all slaves were black and not all nonwhite people were slaves. Throughout the nineteenth century, southern states passed ever more detailed laws defining the acceptable limits of drinking, gambling, and lovemaking along the lines of race and slavery. Those laws attempted to control sites where black and white, slave and free, bargained and socialized freely with one another, places where the white supremacist ideology upon which the defense of slavery increasingly relied was daily undermined in practice. The capstone of the effort to make the categories of race and slavery once again coextensive was the self enslavement laws passed by many states in the 1850s. Based on the racist premise that enslaved people were better off than free people of color because they had white people (read owners) to take care of them, and flirting with the point at which the edifice of pro slavery ideology would collapse beneath the weight of its own absurdity, the laws offered free blacks a chance to choose a master and enslave themselves.' Like many of the other people who came before the courts in cases of disputed racial identity, Alexina Morrison emerged from a shadowy world in which legal and historical categories may have had only episodic relevance to everyday experience. Itwas not unheard of in the antebellum South for people who were legally enslaved to live as free for many years before being dragged into court as slaves.

Nor was it impossible for someone to appear as "black" or, more likely, "mulatto" on one tabulation of the United States census and "white" on another. It sometimes took a long-dormant claim of ownership or an intruding census taker to make people make sense of themselves in the categories that supposedly ordered southern society-black and white, slave and free. When Alexina Morrison escaped from James White, her jailer/protector remembered, the first thing she said was that she was white. And when she brought suit against White, she did so by building this assertion into a story: that she was born of white parents and taken away from her home in Arkansas by "gross fraud," that she had been held by force and falsely claimed as a slave. By the time the case came to trial, however, the pieces of that story had been folded back into the initial assertion of whiteness. Morrison's letters to those whom her lawyers termed "her friends and supposed family" in Arkansas and Texas had gone unanswered (intercepted, the lawyers suggested). As fifteen-year-old Alexina Morrison sat in court while her case was tried, she embodied her lawyer's entire case: her whiteness was "on view ... manifest."Morrison's claim of whiteness drew its power from three sources: her appearance, her behavior, and the idea that "black blood," if present at all, would necessarily be visible. Most simply, her case took the form of outright description. "From his opinion," one witness testified, "the girl is white. Says he judges she is white from her complexion." Or: "Has seen plaintiff and been intimately acquainted with her. From witness' judgment of plaintiff arising from his intimacy she has not the features of the African Race." Other witnesses placed a greater emphasis on behavior when they described what it meant to be white: "Had witness been introduced to the girl without knowing her, he would have taken her for a white girl . . . Has had opportunity of Judging her, and she conducted herself as a white girl. She is so in her conduct and

actions. She has none of the features of an African."
If there had been any of "the African race" in Alexina
Morrison, they argued, it would have been outwardly and
objectively visible in the way she looked and acted,
but from the moment she had made her initial claim of
whiteness, there had been no outward sign that she was
anything but white all the way through. As one witness
put it, on the night when Morrison escaped from the
trader,"she seemed to be in trouble...from her air and
her manners." In other words, she seemed like a white
woman in distress. Alexina Morrison, in her effort to
get free, had been forced to accept attention from
white men, many of them non slaveholders, that went
well beyond their identification with her plight. "Saw
her naked to the waist"-spoken by Morrison's support-
ers, those words circulate through the trial record
like a leitmotiv. Indeed, in the weeks after the mis-
trial, Morrison's half-naked body seems to have been
the center of a festival of whiteness in Jefferson
Parish. P. C. Perret remembered seeing her "frequently"
exhibited at the hotel in Carrollton after the first
trial. And listen to L. Castera, testifying on her behalf and under direct examination in the retrial: "Witness saw the girl at the Hotel and someone asked him if
he thought the girl has African blood, at first witness
answered no, and then made an examination of her nose,
eyes, under her arms, between her shoulders, examined
her hair and the conformation of her face, her fingers,
nails." Or Seaman Hopkins: "examined plaintiff's back
in fact he saw her naked to her waist. Examined her
closely and found no traces of the African." These witnesses, part of an apparently leering and possibly
threatening group of white men, did things to Alexina
Morrison that they would never have done to a white
woman in public, not to a maid, not to a dancing girl,
not to a prostitute. Publicly exhibited, stripped to
the waist, and examined: Alexina Morrison was paying
for her freedom with a performance straight out of the

slave market. For the men at the hotel in Carrollton, Morrison's liminal body, now protected, now violated; now free, now enslaved; now white, now black; now Mexican, now Indian, now Caribbean, was a symbol of everything whiteness promised them: that they would never themselves be slaves, but that they were entitled to benefit from race as slaveholders did from slavery-through control and sexual access. Alexina Morrison had passed from the property regime of slavery into that of whiteness, from being subject to the prerogatives that defined mastery in the antebellum South to being subjected to those that defined white patriarchy. The case was heard in the lower courts for the third time in New Orleans, where, on January 30, 1862, Alexina Morrison was herself "exhibited to the Jury in evidence." Following the instructions of the Supreme Court, the judge admitted the depositions from Arkansas and gave oral instructions to the jury, which were not included in the trial record. After retiring for "some time," the jury sent word that its members were unable to agree upon a verdict and requested that they be allowed to decide by majority. Present in the courtroom, Morrison consented, and the jury returned to announce that it had voted 10 to 2 in her favor. White's lawyers again appealed to the Supreme Court, where the case was delayed during the Civil War occupation of New Orleans, redocketed five days after the assassination of Abraham Lincoln, and continued a few times until 1870, when it was placed on the delay docket where it sits today, apparently awaiting action on Morrison's request for damages. It is tougher to track Alexina Morrison. On the Jefferson Parish census of 1860 she is listed as a free white woman, living with her little girl in a house next door to that of William Dennison, the man whom she had first met as her jailer. Morrison's daughter, like the little girl who lived in Dennison's house, was called Mary. Perhaps one-year-old Mary represented Morrison's shadowed claim to a place within Dennison's household, perhaps, more simply, her daughter was Morrison's best hope for a legacy of freedom. For, by the third hearing of the case (in 1862), Alexina Morrison was apparently back in jail, coughing blood, and fearful for her life. And there the trail ends: Neither Alexina nor Mary Morrison appears in the 1870 census of Jefferson or Orleans parishes. Judged by the history recorded in law books and legislative records and according to the Louisiana Supreme Court that had ultimate jurisdiction over her fate, Morrison was swimming against the current of history, finally unable, in spite of her extraordinary effort, to escape the inexorable consolidation of slave holding power in the years before the Civil War. But if we pay attention to the local as well as the legal importance of the case and the everyday as well as the systemic impact of individual acts of resistance, if we think about what it must have been like to wake up in Jefferson Parish on the morning after the district court had decided Morrison's case and moved on to other business, historical time has a different scale and Alexina Morrison's story offers a different moral. The covering rhetoric of white supremacy may have remained unquestioned and the power of the Supreme Court to dampen subversive appropriations of that rhetoric by refusing the verdicts coming from the lower courts intact. But Alexina Morrison had raised troubling possibilities in a society based on racial slavery: that a slave might perform whiteness so effectively as to become white; that behavior thought to indicate natural difference might, instead, be revealed as the product of education, construction, and, even, commodification; that one could seem white without really being that way; that the whiteness by which the slave holding social order was justified might one day be turned against it. The problems Morrison posed were particularly acute when addressed to the white workingmen who increasingly inhabited the antebellum South: How could they continue to

claim to be their own masters if they or their wives
and daughters worked for someone else? Did race really
give them a stake in slavery? Would their whiteness really protect them from enslavement? No longer could a
Jefferson Parish jury be trusted to try the case of the
slave trader and the white slave; no longer could
slaveholders be sure that the property claims of slavery would be supported by the logic of whiteness. Indeed, the notions of a supposedly commonsense differentiation between black and white that were broach- ed in
the Third District Court were so various and so contra-
dictory that by the end of 1857 it would have been hard
for anyone in Jefferson Parish to say for sure what
people there meant when they talked about "race."
Whether they realized it or not, as they tugged Alexina
Morrison back and forth across a color line that they
all thought they could plainly see, the white partici-
pants in Morrison v. White revealed that line as an effect of social convention and power, not nature."
The Slave Trader, the White Slave, and the Politics of
Racial
 Determination in the 1850s
Author(s): Walter Johnson Source: The Journal of Ameri-
can History, Vol. 87, No. 1 (Jun., 2000), pp. 13-38

Or what about the case of Salome Mueller, born in Al-
sace, Germany in 1813 and brought to America in 1817 by
her father? Salome was separated from her father and
was snatched up by Fritz J. Miller, who had the reputation of "specializing" in kidnapping white people and
selling them as Negros. For 24 years she was held, until someone dug up her birth certificate in Germany.

Another interesting fact, Black people in America owned
so many white people that they had to pass laws forbidding it, "No Negro or Indian though baptized and enjoy-
ing their own freedom shall be capable of any such purchase of (white) Christians, but not yet disbarred from

buying any of their own kind." Act V. Laws of Virginia, Oct 1670.

"No Negro, Mulatto, Indian, although a Christian or any Jew, Mohammedan....shall purchase any Christian White servants."
Act IX. Laws of Virginia Oct 1748

On March 20, 1818, the Louisiana legislature passed similar measures due to the amount of whites being purchased by blacks. In September 1664 Maryland passed a law that if any white woman married a negro, then she would serve the master as well for life. This created a surge in white slave owners encouraging the marrying of white women to blacks so that the white people could be sold legally. It became so prolific that in 1681 they had to pass a law outlawing this practice. The penalty was freedom for the woman and a 10,000 pound tobacco forfeiture.

"And be it further enacted, That no minister of the church of England, or other minister, or person whatsoever, within this colony and dominion, shall hereafter wittingly presume to marry a white man with a negro or mulatto woman; or to marry a white woman with a negro or mulatto man, upon pain of forfeiting and paying, for every such marriage the sum of ten thousand pounds of tobacco; one half to our sovereign lady the Queen, her heirs and successors, for and towards the support of the government, and the contingent charges thereof; and the other half to the informer; To be recovered, with costs, by action of debt, bill, plaint, or information, in any court of record within this her majesty's colony and dominion, wherein no essoin, protection, or wager of law, shall be allowed."

"In the 1640s—before slavery had emerged as an institution in Virginia the colonial legislature, the House of Burgesses, tackled complex questions of servitude and status. The House of Burgesses was elected by the landowners and dominated by the emerging planter class. Their legislation reflected their class interest in controlling the colony's laborers, white and black. From the 1640s through the 1680s, the Burgesses struggled to secure their growing investment in Africans, but at no time was the legislature able to create a certain and clear definition of slaves."

"A 1657 statute regulating runaways also illustrates the lack of any formal recognition of slavery before the 1660s. This law punished runaway servants, who were overwhelmingly European at this time, by extending their service and branding them thus, in 1661, the Burgesses passed its first police regulation of slaves, dealing with the problems of European indentured servants escaping with slaves. To discourage such interracial challenges to the regime, the law provided that Europeans would have to serve extra time for any slaves who ran away with them. The new law declared: in case any English servant shall run away in company of any negroes who are incapable of making satisfaction by addition of a time, it is enacted that the English so running away in the company with them shall at the time of service to their owne masters expired, serve the masters of the said negroes for their absence soe long as they should have done by this act if they had not beene slaves, every christian in company serving his proportion; and if the negroes be lost or dye in such time of their being run away, the christian servants in company with them shall by proportion among them, either pay [four] thousand five hundred pounds of tobacco and caske or [four] yeares service for every negroe soe lost or dead."

"This law not only provided compensation for masters

whose slaves ran away with whites, but also drove a
wedge between African [Aboriginal "Indians" mostly]
slaves and European servants. The colonial legislators
hoped this law would discourage interracial cooperation
and lead it fewer escapes."
italics mines.   Slavery in the United States
Persons or Property? Paul Finkelman p. 108-115.

If you read my previous book, I believe the term
"African" and "Slave" is utilized a bit too loosely,
and if you didn't read it, the here is my position, for
the most part: "Native Americans, including noncombatants, who surrendered during King Philip's War to avoid
enslavement were enslaved at nearly the same rate as
captured combatants, research shows." "Native American
slavery "is a piece of the history of slavery that has
been glossed over," says Linford D. Fisher, associate
professor of history at Brown University. "Between 1492
and 1880, between 2 and 5.5 million Native Americans
were enslaved in the Americas..." "While natives had
been forced into slavery and servitude as early as
1636, it was not until King Philip's War that natives
were enslaved in large numbers, Fisher writes in the
study. The 1675 to 1676 war pitted Native American
leader King Philip, also known as Metacom, and his allies against the English colonial settlers. During the
war, New England colonies routinely shipped Native
Americans as slaves to Barbados, Bermuda, Jamaica, the
Azores, Spain, and Tangier in North Africa, Fisher
says. While Africans who were enslaved did not know
where they would be taken, Native Americans understood
that they could be sent to Caribbean plantations and
face extremely harsh treatment far from their homes and
communities, according to the study. Fear of this fate
spurred some Native Americans to pledge to fight to the
death, while others surrendered hoping to avoid being
sent overseas, the study found. Fisher's study appears
in the journal _Ethnohistory_. Documentation of Native

24

American enslavement shows up in colonial correspondence, shipping records, court cases, town records,
colonial government orders, and petitions from
colonists to the British government."

"Even contemporary official histories of the war all
point to the same thing: Indians were enslaved en masse
and either distributed locally or sent overseas to a
variety of destinations," Fisher writes in the study.
Studies in native slavery have opened up in recent
years, Fisher says, with award-winning books published
in 2002 and 2003 highlighting the systematic nature of
indigenous enslavement, even within English colonies.
Fisher's study on those who surrendered in King
Philip's War looks at what factors contributed to native slavery and the impact enslavement had on Native
Americans for generations."

"Fisher examines the short- and long-term effects of
native slavery in his study, noting that during the
war, the widespread fear of being sold overseas as
slaves was used by Philip-allied Native Americans as a
tool to recruit natives to their side.

Other Native Americans surrendered, Fisher writes, either in response to explicit inducements by the English
offering mercy, or because they hoped that doing so
would be understood as a statement of neutrality. These
surrenders could be individuals, families, larger
bands, or entire communities, Fisher says. Some Native
Americans offered their services to the English in the
war, like Awashonks, the female chief of a confedera-
tion of Sakonnet Indians, who pledged support on the
condition that Sakonnet men, women and children would
not be killed or sent out of the country as slaves, according to the study. Especially near the war's end,
Fisher writes, natives surrendered in larger numbers in
direct response to promises of leniency, but "leniency"
had no consistent, practical meaning. English authori-

ties focused first on disarming natives, either by selling guns turned in by surrenderers or prohibiting them from bearing arms, Fisher writes. English communities objected to letting natives who surrendered simply go free, and housing and feeding them was complicated, so often captured and surrendered Native Americans were simply sold into slavery, both overseas and within New England, or forced into servitude for limited terms within English households. In addition, native communities were asked to pay an annual tribute of five shillings per male "as an acknowledgment of their subjection" to the government of Connecticut, according to the study. New Englanders' motivations for enslaving Native Americans included making money and clearing land for colonists to claim, Fisher writes. It was also easier to remove Native Americans from the region than to sell them locally and risk having the Native Americans run away to find refuge. Fisher also argues that there was an ideological component to enslaving Native Americans. Among colonists, "there was a presumption involving the innate inferiority of natives," he says. "There were proto-racial notions of European superiority, plus an appetite for land," he says. "If you look at the history of the colonies, slavery happens almost right away." Fisher says he is increasingly convinced that, for colonists, "slavery was a normal part of their mental framework." Some free Native Americans working with the English tried to influence where Native American surrenderers would be settled and how they would be treated, Fisher writes, like Uncas, the sachem of the Mohegans in Connecticut. Uncas, who fought on the side of the English, "seemed determined postwar to keep Indians out of English households and—even more important—off of English merchant ships that threatened to take them to the Caribbean," Fisher writes. Uncas and other Native Americans also encouraged captives to run away and sheltered them when they did, or helped them resettle elsewhere, according to the study. In other cases, Fisher writes, Native Americans requested captives as servants for themselves, sometimes to keep them out of English households, or served as slave-trading middlemen. In one case, Fisher notes, a Native American slave owned by a Pequot leader was sold by him to an enslaved African woman."

"The shadow of native enslavement in New England extends into the 18th century and beyond," Fisher says. "There are records of people petitioning for freedom in the 1740s who were the descendants of Native Americans first enslaved during King Philip's War." In the study, he writes, "Small legal loopholes and dishonest practices on the ground ensured that, in many cases, limited-term service turned into lifelong and even heritable slavery." In 1676, Connecticut officials decreed that a native slave's term of service could be lengthened but not shortened. A law passed the same year by the Rhode Island General Assembly seemed on the surface to outlaw Indian slavery, but, Fisher notes, in practice that and other laws ensured that Native surrenderers were "disposed of" for the benefit of the colony, with various terms of servitude. For Native Americans five years of age or younger, their servitude lasted until they were 30 years old. These enslavement practices permanently disrupted the "lives, livelihoods, and kinship networks of thousands of Indians," Fisher writes, and sometimes slavery was simply given another name."

"In 1721, 45 years after the end of King Philip's War, the Connecticut General Assembly took up the question of second-generation Native American child slaves. The Native American children who had been placed as servants in English households after the war had grown up and had children of their own. What should be done with them? Fisher writes that while leaders did not approve of enslaving them, they also did not want to set them free, so that generation of children also became indentured servants. Native Americans sold overseas occasionally made it back to the United States, Fisher writes. Others died or disappeared into a wider slave market and labor force, or became established in the locations where they were sent, like the modern-day community of individuals in Bermuda who claim New England Indian descent."

[Brown University] —A study by Linford D. Fisher, associate professor of history at Brown University, finds that Native Americans, including noncombatants, who surrendered during King Philip's War to avoid enslavement were enslaved at nearly the same rate as captured combatants.

But not just during King Phillip's War, this was part and parcel with every expansion of colonial territory, the aboriginals would be kidnapped and sold as slaves. The "African slave trade" is the cover story. Yes, some slaves did come from Africa, but the majority were already here. White people, "Indians," Mexicans, Blacks or anyone who was out and about could be kidnapped and sold into slavery. Again, they were killing parents and stealing their children to sell, they were kidnapping white people, dying them brown, they were capturing people like animals and selling them as such. It was business. White people, especially females, today have forgotten, they feel safe now, but there was a time when they were scurrying around, like everyone else, dodging the "slavers" right here in America and Europe. Labor, sexual exploitation and all manner of indignities was the penalty for being in the wrong place, at the right time, whatever your hue.

"From the start of the 17th century to the early 19th century, between one half and two thirds of all the White colonists who came to the New World came as slaves. They were owned as property, were accorded no rights and had no recourse to the law. Laws relating to fugitive black slaves also applied to them.

Most books on white labour in early American history referrer to these people as "indentured servitude" or "bondservants." The reality, however, is that the conditions these people lived and worked under should more properly be termed as permanent slavery unto death. The papers allowing the enslavement, termed indentures, were often forged by kidnappers and press-gangs. The owner of the indentured worker had the right to increase the length of the term of indenture, in reality making it a life sentence, on the flimsiest of excuses. The "indentured worker" had no say in the matter. Although these people are not called "slaves" today, perhaps for political rather than historical reasons, people at the time had no qualms about using the word to describe these people. In Thomas Burton's Parliamentary Diary 1656-1659, in 1659 the English parliament debated the practice of selling Britons into slavery in the New World. In the Calendar of State Papers, Colonial Series, America and West Indies of 1701, there is a passage that tells of a protest over the "encouragement to the spiriting away of Englishmen without their consent and selling them for slaves, which hath been a practice very frequent and known by the name of kidnapping." In the British West Indies, plantation slavery had begun as early as 1627. In Barbados by the 1640's there were an estimated 25,000 slaves; 21,700 of these slaves were white. The word "kidnapping" itself comes from the expression "kid-nabbing", which referred to the practice of abducting children to be sold in the British factories or into plantation slavery in America. Another phrase that has its roots in white slavery is "spirited away" because white slavers that kidnapped fellow whites were called "spirits."

"The British newspaper, The Argosy, reported in 1893 that "Few, but readers of old colonial state papers and records, are aware that between the years 1649 to 1690 a lively trade was carried on between England and the plantations, as the colonies were then called, [a trade] in political prisoners… they were sold at auction… for various terms of years, sometimes for life, as slaves." "The situation of the white slaves in the New World echoed that of the conditions of worker in Britain during this period. Their legal form of contracted indentured servitude was little better than common slavery. British children were routinely taken from orphanages and workhouses to be put in factories for a lifetime of horrors. They often worked 16-hour days of unceasing toil, without a break. If they dared to fall asleep at their machines, they were whipped awake. For committing crimes such as arriving late or talking during work, they were beaten with a "billy-roller," an eight feet long by one and a half inch diameter iron bar. The primitive machines in the factories mutilated thousands of children each year. Often disabled for life by these accidents, they were simply turned out onto the street.

What must also be considered is that when these "free" workers didn't have enough food to eat, they simply starved. Their bosses didn't care if they lived or died or about the conditions they lived in. There was an endless supply of workers from the local area who could and would replace them. Black slaves in America, however, were an investment for the slave owner. He had paid for them so it was in his interests to insure that his investment was kept functional. This meant that in terms of diet, health and shelter, black slaves in America were often better off than white "workers" in the north of America and actually far better off than workers in much of industrialized Europe."

Slavery and White Guilt -By James Eden: 21st August 2013 UK.

It is also important to place this activity in context with the ongoing business of slavery in other parts of the world. While all were being scooped up in the Americas, white folks were also being scooped up in Europe and the Mediterranean by the Moors. The Moors had a history of navigation, long before the colonial powers became prominent, the Moors had sailed the seas as traders, merchants and slavers. To the Moors, the poor Whites, Whites taken in raids and white folks period it was open season, especially young White Women. Just as in America, the Moors viewed the lesser, those outside of its construct, as chattel animals, especially given the historical interaction between the Moorish empire and Europe. Much attention and condemnation has been directed towards the tragedy of the slave trade which took place during the 16-19th centuries. However, another equally despicable trade in humans was taking place around the same time in the Mediterranean. It is estimated that up to 1.25 million Europeans were enslaved by the so-called Barbary corsairs (Moors), and their lives were just as pitiful as their African counterparts. They have come to be known as the white slaves of Barbary. Slavery is one of the oldest trades known to man. We can first find records of the slave trade dating back to The Code of Hammurabi in Babylon in the 18th century BCE. People from virtually every major culture, civilization, and religious background have made slaves of their own and enslaved other peoples. However, comparatively little attention has been given to the prolific slave trade that was carried out by pirates, or corsairs(MOORS), along the Barbary coast (as it was called by Europeans at the time), in what is now Morocco, Algeria, Tunisia, and Libya, beginning around 1600 AD. "Anyone traveling in the Mediterranean at the time faced the real prospect of being captured by the Corsairs and taken to Barbary Coast cities and being sold as slaves. However, not content with attacking ships and sailors, the corsairs also sometimes raided coastal settlements in Italy, France, Spain, Portugal, England, Ireland, and even as far away as the Netherlands and Iceland. They landed on unguarded beaches, and crept up on villages in the dark to capture their victims. Almost all the inhabitants of the village of Baltimore, in Ireland, were taken in this way in 1631. As a result of this threat, numerous coastal towns in the Mediterranean were almost completely abandoned by their inhabitants until the 19 [th] century. In the 13th and 14th centuries, it was Christian pirates, primarily from Catalonia and Sicily, that dominated the seas, posing a constant threat to merchants. It was not until the expansion of the Ottoman Empire in the 15 [th] century that the Barbary corsairs started to become a menace to Christian shipping. Around 1600 AD, European pirates brought advanced sailing and shipbuilding techniques to the Barbary Coast, which enabled the corsairs to extend their activities into the Atlantic Ocean, and the impact of Barbary raids peaked in the early to mid-17th century. While the Barbary slave trade is typically portrayed as Muslim corsairs capturing white Christian victims, this is far too simplistic. In reality, the corsairs were not concerned with the race or religious orientation of those they captured. Slaves in Barbary could be black, brown or white, Catholic, Protestant, Orthodox, Jewish or Muslim. And the corsairs were not only Muslim; English privateers and Dutch captains also exploited the changing loyalties of an era in which friends could become enemies and enemies friends with the stroke of a pen."

"One of the things that both the public and many scholars have tended to take as given is that slavery was always racial in nature," said historian Robert Davis, author of *Christian Slaves, Muslim Masters: White Slavery in the Mediterranean, the Barbary Coast, and Italy* . "But that is not true," he added."

"In comments which may stoke controversy, Davis claims that white slavery had been minimized or ignored because academics preferred to treat Europeans as evil

colonialists rather than as victims. The slaves captured by the Barbary pirates faced a grim future. Many
died on the ships during the long voyage back to North
Africa due to disease or lack of food and water. Those
who survived were taken to slave markets where they
would stand for hours while buyers inspected them before they were sold at auction. After purchase, slaves
would be put to work in various ways. Men were usually
assigned to hard manual labour, such as working in
quarries or heavy construction, while women were used
for housework or in sexual servitude. At night the
slaves were put into prisons called 'bagnios' that were
often hot and overcrowded. However, by far the worst
fate for a Barbary slave was being assigned to man the
oars of galleys. Rowers were shackled where they sat,
and never allowed to leave. Sleeping, eating, defeca-
tion and urination took place at the seat. Overseers
would crack the whip over the bare backs of any slaves
considered not to be working hard enough."

The White Slaves of Barbary-April Holloway

@ancient-origins.net 10/6/2014

"The battles and raids of the Iberian reconquest and
its aftermath inevitably yielded prisoners. And just as
inevitably these prisoners were considered to be part
of the booty of their captors. Those who could afford
to redeem themselves by paying their ransom did so.
Those who could not were sold into slavery. It is important to realize how generic a process this was in
the Mediterranean world as a whole and, more specifically, in Spain, where, from the twelfth century on,
the frontier between Christendom and Islam was so unstable. Even after the mid thirteenth century, when the
Muslim threat was more or less confined to North
Africa, the raids (and hence the captures and ransoms)
continued, though now primarily on the sea rather than
on land. The elaborate structures that developed on
both the Iberian and North African sides of the straits

to deal with the ransoming of captives testify to the "business as usual" nature of the process." The early thirteenth century even saw the emergence of the Mercedarian Order in the Crown of Aragon, whose principal function it was to raise money to expedite the release of captives whose financial circumstances did not permit them to take advantage of traditional avenues of redemption."

The "Moors" of West Africa and the Beginnings of the Portuguese Slave Trade Kenneth Baxter Wolf   1-1-1994 Pomona College p. 14.

So while America was busy being formed into a corporate structure, kidnapping and all, the world had been kidnapping for centuries peoples of all colors. Is it not to be expected that it would be open season of Whites in America? Why somehow has this fact been excluded from basic education? Why aren't White people told, ad nausem, that they were slaves in Europe, in Africa and in America? This small omission is huge. To better understand how the Moor's will play a role in America's slavery, one has to go back and study a brief history of the Moor's. I tried to find the oldest and condensed version that I could, the older, the better. The Moors, keep in mind, were a lot of things, but they primarily were slavers, and the most valuable slave in that part of the world was Whites, and especially women. The significance of the Moor's will become apparent later, but one has to understand the history of this empire in order to fast forward to the present, in order to shatter some of the myths that have crippled the psyche of Whites and Blacks in America. One must look at the real historical economic drivers.

The Moorish empire was not the only slavers of White people. One of the largest places for the sale of White slaves was Crimea.

"When we think of slavery, we tend to think of this African traffic. Yet it was not the only such trade – nor was it, before 1700, even the largest. A second great market in slaves once sullied the world, this one less well-known, vastly longer-lasting, and centred on the Black Sea ports of the Crimea. It was a huge trade in its own right; in its great years, which lasted roughly from 1200 until 1760, an estimated 6.5 million prisoners were shipped off to new and often intensely miserable lives in places ranging from Italy to India. Slavery in the Crimea, however, differed in significant ways from the model made so familiar by the trans-Atlantic trade. The slaves sold there were drawn for the most part from the great plains of the Ukraine and southern Russia in annual raids known as the "harvesting of the steppe." Their masters were successively Vikings, Italians and Tatars – the latter being, for nearly half of the trade's life, the subjects of the Crimean Khanate, a state that owed its own long life to its ability to satisfy demand for slaves. And most of the slaves themselves were not male labourers. They were women and children destined for domestic service – a fate that not infrequently included sexual service. The latter sort of slave was always fairly commonplace in the Crimea. When the Ottoman writer Evliea Celebi toured the north shores of the Black Sea in 1664, he noted down some examples of the local dialect that he hoped other travelers to the region might find useful. Among the phrases that Çelebi selected were "Bring a girl" and "I found no girl, but I found a boy." This special focus – in a market that lay at the intersection not only of Europe and Asia, but also of Christianity and Islam – produced remarkable consequences. More women than men were put up for sale in the Crimea, and they consistently fetched higher prices. The high value of females was established at a very early date – articles 110-121 of the twelfth century *Russkaia Pravda*, the oldest known Russian law code, noted that female slaves were worth more than males - and it persisted throughout the entire history of the Black Sea trade. Female slaves were twice as expensive as males in Crete in 1301 and 60 percent more expensive 30 years later; when a Turkish noble, Kenan Bey, wrote his will around 1600, a slave girl he left to his wife turned out to be his single most valuable piece of property. As a result, as many as 80 percent of all Black Sea slaves whose sexes and ages are known were females aged between 8 and 24. The slave traders of the Crimean Khanate became expert at manipulating their stocks so that they could offer Christian slaves to Muslim customers and Muslim slaves to Christians. They became connoisseurs of their clients' widely varying tastes in beauty. And they developed a fine appreciation of the value of exoticism. Among the most highly-priced slaves on sale in the Crimean markets were blacks from sub-Saharan Africa, who found a ready market in all-white Muscovy, and Circassians from the Caucasus – famed even then for their beauty. The most prized of all varieties of slave, however, appear to have been children brought all the way to the Crimea from the far north – boys and girls who were perhaps between six and 13 years old, who had been seized in organized raids on the Finnish district of Karelia, and then trafficked south via Novgorod, Moscow, and the Dnieper. So valuable were children of this sort – and so likely, therefore, to be bought and sold along the way – that only a handful of Finnish exotics ever found their way to the Crimea; Jukka Korpela estimates that their numbers may have been as low as half a dozen a year. The prices they commanded, however, were simply colossal; one source notes that girls who could be purchased for as little as 5 *altyn* in Karelia could be resold for 6,666 *altyn* even before they reached the Khanate- a mark up in excess of 133,000 percent. The higher price, equivalent to 200 roubles or (in about 1600) 250 sheep, was also about five times the usual price for a Crimean slave. It is no surprise, in these circumstances, that slaves from the far north were highly sought-after for their coloring – nor that their special characteristics were scrupulously noted in the slave registers so carefully kept in the ports that lay at the heart of this commerce in human misery: "white skin, white hair." To get some idea of how this slave trade worked, how it developed and how it was made profitable, it is necessary first to make the point that slave raiding and slave trading were the economic mainstays of the Crimea throughout the medieval period. The trade actually rose and fell twice, once before and once after the fall of Constantinople in 1453, demand for pagan or Muslim slaves for Byzantium being supplanted by the market for Christian slaves in the Ottoman Empire. There seem to have been few years in this period, however, in which at least 2,000 prisoners were not shipped out of Caffa, a port which Mikhalon Litvin – a Lithuanian writing in about 1550 – described as "not a town, but an abyss into which our blood is pouring." That figure, moreover, substantially understates the true extent of slavery in the Crimea. It has been estimated that at least a third of the prisoners brought into the peninsula remained there, working as slaves for Tatar masters. Another substantial group found their way to rival ports in the peninsula, or were sold on to buyers from other Mongol successor-states such as the khanates of Kazan and Astrakhan. The Crimean Khanate and its immediate neighbours in 1600. Understanding this mechanics of this fearsomely efficient business means understanding its parameters. The first and most significant of these was geography. The steppe, which ran uninterrupted from Mongolia all the way to Hungary and Poland, provided the forage required by mounted raiding parties while offering no significant barriers to either the rapid movement of large groups of horsemen or their swift retreat. Neither the great Polish Lituanian Commonwealth (which was until the 1660s the major power in eastern Europe) nor its weaker neighbor, Muscovy, had a defined southern border; rather, both states had frontiers, which were almost impossible to seal. Fortifications were introduced at several spots from the late sixteenth century, but it was not until the 1640s that the Muscovites began the long process of building the Belgorod Line, a chain of forts, earth ramparts and long lines of felled trees that eventually ran for 800 kilometres. These defenses limited the Tatars' freedom of movement, and eventually (though not until the 1760s) rendered large-scale raids impossible. Before that date, however, raiding parties ranged more or less at will across the endless steppe, burning villages, seizing captives, and dragging them off to the south along familiar routes labeled on seventeenth century maps as the "black roads" of the slave trade. What was it like to be one of those prisoners? There is no one answer to that question. The truth seems to be that, in certain circumstances, being a slave was not intolerable. Male captives sent to work, chained, in the galleys – a common enough fate in those days –endured lives that were about as hard as it is possible to imagine. For others, though, slavery meant being clothed and housed and fed, and often it meant household work rather than the backbreaking physical toil expected of a steppe peasant. Captivity of this variety was not too far removed from the sort of life endured by an indentured servant who signed a long term contract promising to serve a single master for a paltry wage, plus board and lodging. In one telling anecdote dating to the last days of the Black Sea trade, a party of miserably impoverished Circassians held on board a ship headed for Istanbul was freed by the crew of a Russian naval vessel. Given the choice of a return home, marriage to Russian or Cossack men, or remaining with their Turkish slave-master, "unanimously and without a moment's consideration, they exclaimed, 'To Constantinople – to be sold!'"In the better-regulated Muslim lands, moreover, slavery was not necessarily for life. Some slaves secured their freedom after a quarter of a century – one English traveler in central Asia stumbled across a party of 25 freed Russian slaves heading home from Samarkand – and captives who married rarely passed on their slave status to their children, as was certainly the case in the Atlantic trade. Those who had good looks, luck and talent might make something of themselves in circumstances such as these. Perhaps the most celebrated example of a slave who rose far above her humble origins was that of Aleksandra Lisowska, the able daughter of a Ruthenian priest who was seized by the Crimean Tatars in Galicia during the 1520s. Taken to Caffa and then sold on to Istanbul, she became the favourite wife of the Turkish sultan Suleiman the Magnificent and a significant power in her own right in the Ottoman Empire. It would be a terrible mistake, however, to see the Crimean slave trade as in any sense benign. Capture by a Tatar raiding party could and often did mean death. The very young and very old -those unable to walk – would be released or simply killed at this point. An account by Sigmund Freiherr von Herberstein, an envoy from the Holy Roman Empire who visited Russia in the sixteenth century, alleged that "old and infirm men, who will not fetch much at a sale, are given up to the Tartar youths much as hares are given to whelps by way of their first lesson in hunting." The respective fates of the young and attractive and of those too old to work are confirmed by a snatch of Ukrainian folk song: "Old mother is sacred -And my dear is taken into captivity." Those who were fit and beautiful enough to survive this cull would have their hands pinioned behind their backs and be yoked in lines to Tatar ponies. Secured in this fashion, and whipped to ensure that they maintained a steady pace behind their captors, they would trudge for several hundred miles across the steppe. Male prisoners were sometimes castrated and frequently branded, and those who survived both this harsh treatment and the march south were confined in Crimean dungeons, classified according to their age, sex, status and skills, and finally inspected for physical appearance. Here the experience of slaves seems to have been humiliatingly similar throughout the long years of the eastern trade. Writing in the 1420s, the Spanish traveler Pero Tafur recorded that the Genoese forced new slaves to "strip to the skin, males as well as females, and they put on them a cloak of felt, and the price is named. Afterwards they throw off their coverings and make them walk up and down to show whether they have any bodily defect." 250 years later, so many Tatar slavers used cosmetics to improve the appearance of their female captives that the Khanate issued an edict forbidding the practice. The Crimean Khan Devlet I Giray, who reigned over the slave state at the height of its power between 1551 and 1577, receives a group of western ambassadors. The value of these captives varied significantly over the years according to both the numbers coming onto the market and the personal qualities of the slaves themselves. General factors, especially the advent of war and peace, famine and epidemics, made huge differences to cost, and this seems to have remained true irrespective of which power was in control of the Black Sea slave routes. We know that, in the last days of the Byzantine Empire, when the Crimean trade was in the hands of the Genoese and the Venetians, prices rose sharply as a result of a severe outbreak of plague in Romania in 1393, and also that in the closing years of the thirteenth century the price of a Turkish slave fell briefly below that of a sheep thanks to the glut of prisoners produced by a successful Byzantine campaign. Similarly, during a famine in Astrakhan in the 1550s, peasants would sell their daughters into slavery for six pence worth of corn. Four decades later, in a time of plenty, girl slaves in the same town cost 405 florints. Specifics mattered a great deal, too, however. Noble captives taken during military campaigns would be ransomed rather than sold on the open market. When János Kemény, the Prince of Transylvania, was captured in 1658 with a number of his nobles, he was eventually ransomed for 100,000 thalers (a quarter of what had originally been demanded) and a subordinate, Ferenc Kornis, for 40,000. A surviving register of prisoners lists 275 other named captives, and of these a further 66 are known to have been ransomed for an additional 64,530 thalers – a total figure equivalent to eight years' of tribute payments by the Transylvanians. A Crimean Tatar warrior, wielding the celebrated recurved bow that was for centuries the main weapon of the Mongol and Tatar peoples. Raiding parties of such warriors, up to 30,000 strong, scoured the western steppes for prisoners almost annually throughout the medieval and early modern periods. By the seventeenth century, moreover, ransoms were increasingly being paid for far less exalted captives. Redeeming prisoners from the clutches of the infidel had come to be regarded in both Muscovy and Poland-Lithuania as a moral and religious duty – no Christian could view with anything less than horror the fate of slaves who died in Muslim lands without administration of the last rites – and it was because of this that Muscovy collected a special ransom tax to redeem thousands of ordinary prisoners between 1551 and 1679. There is also good evidence that all Crimean captives were the subject of elaborate pricing mechanisms; the usual prices charged for slaves were, for example, discounted to take account of physical imperfections and injuries. A case tried in Genoa in 1423 concerned a Bulgar slave girl who had been struck over the head when she was captured and now suffered from "falling sickness" – perhaps epilepsy. The slave-owner was able to press a case to get the sale declared invalid on the grounds that the girl had been ill at the time he purchased her. Finally, it is important to see the eastern slave trade in its proper context. To think

of the Muscovites and Poles as nothing more than victims of the Tatars is to radically distort the truth.
Muscovy, in particular, was frequently complicit, and
the institution of slavery flourished for many years
within its borders. This was a matter of special significance when it comes to explaining how it was possible for Finns to find their way to the Crimean market,
for the truth is that they were mostly seized and sent
there by Russians. The northern town of Novgorod –
known during the middle ages as Novgorod the Great in
deference to its wealth and power – was a key centre of
the slave trade in this region, and the men of Novgorod
are known to have mounted numerous raids into Karelia
with the explicit purpose of capturing exotic Finnish
children. Prisoners taken in this region were so valuable, indeed, that after the incorporation of the
Khanate of Astrakhan into the growing Muscovite empire,
the son of its former khan was permitted to lead two
expeditions through Muscovy to launch raids in Karelia
(1555 and 1577), while Shah Abbas of Persia sent dele-
gations that managed to acquire three Finnish girls in
Moscow and 30 more in Kazan. Life for forest Finns.
This 1893 oil painting by Eero Jarnefelt is a late rep-
resentation of an age-old way of life that had probably
changed little since the days that Tatars from Astrakhan traveled half way across west Asia to raid the
country for blonde children. The advantages of slave
raiding in the far north were considerable. There was
no powerful Finnish state capable of protecting its
subjects, and although most southern parts of Finland
were Christianize during the Middle Ages, large swathes
of the population remained pagan – an attractive proposition, since captives from this source enjoyed no protection from the church and could be sold indiscrimi-
nately to both Christian and Muslim buyers. The proxim-
ity of Novgorod meant that there was a major slaving
base nearby, and removed much of the cost and risk involved in transporting prisoners across large dis-

42

tances. According to Jukka Korpela, the chronicles of the medieval period record major raids into Karelia on average once every 10 years between the mid-14th and early 16th centuries, "which is a very high frequency in view of the fact that this area lay outside the interests of the late medieval realms." Some were mounted by private enterprise – notably "marauding boatmen" from Novgorod. Others were sponsored by local rulers who hoped to profit handsomely from them. This petroglyph, showing Karelian skiers, is one of the earliest surviving representations of the Finnish people. The earliest records that we have of Muscovite raids in this region date to 1477, the year before Novgorod fell to Tsar Ivan the Great. An account dating to 1490 gives more detail about the specifics of the trade: the Russians plundered the parish of Kemi, in northern Finland, kidnapped its women and children, and offered them for ransom. Some families paid to recover their relatives; most could not, and lost them to slavery. When Tatar troops from Astrakhan mounted their similar raid in 1577, they left children too young to walk out on the ice to die. This trade in Scandinavian captives – known to the Muscovites as *nemtsy* – flourished throughout the 16th century, and was large enough for other rulers to send specially to Moscow for these coveted slaves. Izmail-bek, the khan of the Nogai horde (whose lands were situated north of the Crimea) sent a diplomat north to purchase two Scandinavian children in 1561; the khan of far-off Bukhara dispatched a delegation which toured the slave quarters of five towns for *nemtsy* girls. The prices they paid were about ten times the average for an ordinary slave, and Korpela suggests that the word *nemtsy* itself became practically a trademark, "which referred to an already established extra quality." While the numbers of Finnish captives who actually reached the Crimea was undoubtedly low, therefore, the fact that there was plainly an active trade in them, involving special terminology, a long-distance trading network, and — last but by no means least — clear profits, suggests a sophistication and an ability to disseminate intelligence and even place "orders" for slaves with particularly valued characteristics that seem remarkable at such an early date. The Karelian taiga, location of several centuries of slave raid that distributed highly-valued Finnish children throughout much of Asia. It can be argued, indeed, that the significance of the Crimean slave trade as a whole has been severely under-estimated. It was not simply a precursor of the Atlantic trade; it provided a model and, in a number of cases, the expertise for it. Some of the Genoese slavers who were thrown out of Caffa by the Ottomans a few years after the fall of Byzantium reappeared as founders of the Atlantic trade towards the end of the fifteenth century. Moreover, Ottoman Istanbul, the largest city in all of Europe and western Asia by 1550, grew rapidly in part because one in five of its booming population was a Crimean slave. And the Cossacks of the Ukraine first organised themselves into large bands to protect against Tatar slave raids. Finally, the diversion of Muscovite resources and Russian gold to Caffa plainly had some impact on the development of Russia. The cost of ransom slavery alone was as much as 6 million roubles each year after 1600, and the great Russian historian Vasily Klyuchevsky — writing late in the nineteenth century, at a time when Russia's inability to keep pace with the developing west was a matter of prime political importance — observed that "if you consider how much time and spiritual and material strength was wasted in the monotonous, brutal, toilsome and painful pursuit of [the Tatar] steppe predators, one need not ask what people in Eastern Europe were doing while those of Western Europe advanced in industry and commerce, in civil life and in the arts and sciences." That so many lives, and so many millions in gold, in short, were not available to be invested in Russia, nor to be directed against Poland-Lithuania or

Sweden for so long, may have been merely an inadvertent consequence of the Crimean khan's inability to control his chiefs and followers. It *was* a consequence, nonetheless."

Sources: https://mikedashhistory.com/2015/01/15/blonde-cargoes-finnish-children-in-the-slave-markets-of-medieval-crimea/ Eric Christiansen. *The Northern Crusades*. London: Macmillan, 1980; Virgil Ciocîltan. *The Mongols and the Black Sea Trade in the Thirteenth and Fourteenth Centuries*. Leiden: Brill, 2012; Leslie J.D. Collins. *The Fall of Shaikh Ahmed Khan and the Fate of the People of the Great Horde, 1500-1504*. Unpublished University of London PhD thesis, 1970; Jodocus Crull. *The Ancient and Present State of Muscovy*. London: A. Roper, 1698; David Brion Davis. *Inhuman Bondage: The Rise and Fall of Slavery in the New World*. Oxford: Oxford University Press, 1996; David Eltis. *The Rise of African Slavery in the Americas*. Cambridge: Cambridge University Press, 2000; David Eltis and David Richardson. *Atlas of the Transatlantic Slave Trade*. New Haven: Yale University Press, 2010; Maria Ivanics. 'Enslavement, slave labour and the treatment of captives in the Crimean Khanate.' In Géza Dávid and Pál Fodor (eds). *Ransom Slavery along the Ottoman Borders*. Leiden: Koninklijke Brill, 2007; Kate Fleet. *European and Islamic Trade in the Early Ottoman State: the Merchants of Genoa and Turkey*. Cambridge: Cambridge University Press, 2004; Charles J. Halperin. *The Tatar Yoke: The Image of the Mongols in Medieval Russia*. Bloomington [IN]: Slavica Publishers, 2009; Richard Hellie. *Slavery in Russia 1450-1725*. Chicago: University of Chicago Press, 1982; V. L. Ianin. 'Medieval Novgorod.' in *The Cambridge History of Russia: From Early Rus' to 1689*. Cambridge: Cambridge University Press, 2008; Halil Inalcik. 'The Khan and the tribal aristocracy: the Crimean Khanate under Sahib Giray I.' *Harvard Ukrainian Studies* 3-4 (1979-80); Michael Khoradovsky. *Russia's*

Steppe Frontier: The Making of a Colonial Empire, 1500-1800. Bloomington: Indianapolis University Press, 2002; Mikhail Kililov. 'Slave trade in the early modern Crimea from the perspective of Christian, Muslim and Jewish sources.' *Journal of Early Modern History* 11 (2007); Charles King. *The Black Sea: A History*. Oxford: Oxford University Press, 2005; Denise Klein (ed). *The Crimean Khanate Between East and West (15th-18th Century)*. Wiesbaden: Harrassowitz, 2012; D. Kolodziejczyk. 'Slave hunting and slave redemption as a business enterprise: the northern Black Sea region in the sixteenth to seventeenth centuries.' *Oriente Moderno* 86 (2006); Jukka Korpela. 'The Baltic Finnic People in the Medieval and Pre-Modern Eastern European Slave Trade.' *Russian History* 41 (2014); Eizo Matsuki, "The Crimean Tatars and their Russian-Captive Slaves: an Aspect of Muscovite-Crimean Relations in the 16th and 17th Centuries", Mediterranean Studies Group at Hitotsubashi University, nd; Alexandre Skirda. *La Traite des Slaves: L'Escalvage des Blancs du VIII au XVIII Siècle*. Paris: Les Editions de Paris Max Chaleil, 2010; Alessandro Stanziani. *Bondage: Labor and Rights in Eurasia from the Sixteenth to the Early Twentieth Centuries*. New York: Berghahn Books, 2014; William Urban, 'Victims of the Baltic Crusade.' *Journal of Baltic Studies* 29 (1998); Charles Verlinden. 'Medieval "Slavers".' In David Herlihy, Robert S. Lopez and Vsevolod Slessarev (eds.), *Economy, Society and Government in Medieval Italy*, Kent [OH]: Kent State University Press, 1969; Brian Glyn Williams. *The Crimean Tatars: The Diaspora Experience and the Forging of a Nation*. Leiden: Brill, 2001.

Again, slavery was like crack in the 80's in Los Angeles. The Moors, the Russians, the Americans, and everyone in between were engaged in the slave trade and race did not matter. In American textbooks school students are led to believe that it was only Africa and only

America involved in the slave trade, and that it was only Blacks who were slaves. We have established that slavery was a global business, we have established that White folks were kidnapped and sold as slaves in America, and we have established the rise and fall of the Moorish empire, who were, among- st other things, slavers. All of this is relevant how? Well, we have to start with the founding of America and George Washington. George Washington was the field Marshall for an international cartel of businessmen who concocted a plot to generate revenue by the overthrow of the British rule in the colonies and America.

GEORGE WASHINGTON and Ben Franklin-

While most of the history books paint a nice wholesome
portrait of Washington, reality is a bit more sobering.
In order to understand Washington, one has to understand the economic schisms of that "colonial" period.
Again, worldwide slavery was crack, always keep that
in mind when you view colonial periods, because slave
labor was what produced the revenue, from actual
slaves, to agriculture, inter alia, mining, construction and ranching. George Washington was close friends
with Thomas Jefferson and Ben Franklin. Ben Franklin
was a master of propaganda, publisher of newspapers,
close confidant of France, the City of London and fo-
menter of the regime change we now call the American
Revolution. Remember, the Virginia Company of London
had already been in America since the early 1600s,

"The Virginia Company of London By the early 17th century, England was one of the leading European powers involved in trans-oceanic trade and was beginning to
build a colonial empire. Wealthy merchants, eager to
find investment opportunities, established a number of
companies set up to trade in various parts of the
world. Each company, made up of individuals who purchased shares of company stock, was given a monopoly to
explore, trade or settle a particular region of the
world. Profits were shared among the investors according to the amount of stock they owned. Between 1575 and
1630, more than 6,300 Englishmen and women invested in
joint stock companies trading with Russia, Turkey,
Africa, the East Indies, the Mediterranean and America.
England's first successful colony in America was not
established by the English government, but by one of
these privately-owned businesses called the Virginia
Company of London. Investors in the Virginia Company
hoped to profit from the wealth of the New World. In
1606 King James I granted the Company organizers exclu-

sive rights to settle in Virginia. Their mission was to extend the bounds of English civilization by finding wealth, converting the Virginia Indians to Christianity, creating jobs for England's unemployed, seeking a route to the Orient, and tapping the resources of the New World. The first leader of the Virginia Company in England was its treasurer, Sir Thomas Smythe. A charter granted land to two branches of the Company—the London branch was to settle a colony near the Chesapeake Bay, while the Plymouth branch was granted land in the New England area. The Company paid all the costs of establishing each colony, and in return controlled all land and resources there and required everyone to work for the Company. Investors, called "adventurers," purchased shares of stock to help finance the costs of establishing overseas settlements. Money from the sale of stock was used to pay for ships and supplies and to recruit and outfit laborers. A single share of stock in the Virginia Company cost 12 pounds 10 shillings, the equivalent of over six month's wages for an ordinary working man. In an extensive publicity campaign, the Company circulated pamphlets, plays, sermons and broadsides throughout England to raise interest in New World investments. Shareholders could buy stock individually or in groups. Almost 1700 people purchased shares, including men of different occupations and classes, wealthy women, and representatives of institutions such as trade guilds, towns and cities. The largest single investor was Thomas West, Lord de la Warr, who served as the first governor of Virginia between 1610 and 1618. The idea of colonization appealed to all classes of English society. Members of the gentry were interested in the glory of having overseas colonies, hoping to spread England's fame abroad and frustrate Spanish ambitions in the New World. Merchants hoped to develop new industries that would provide essential goods and resources and eliminate England's dependence upon imports from European countries. They also hoped that

colonies could provide a market for English goods.
Poorer members of the population hoped to improve their
lot, with the possibility of jobs and the opportunity
to acquire land. Supplying an overseas colony with
food, materials and laborers was an expensive venture
for the Virginia Company, and it depended upon the sale
of stock to raise money. The idea of owning shares of
stock in a Company to get wealthy is not a new idea.
But when not enough people were willing to take the
risk and buy stock, Company officials turned to another
money-making idea that is not new either—running lotteries. The Company organized lotteries in London and
outlying towns, with prizes of up to 5,000 pounds sterling. These lotteries soon became the primary source of
investment income for the Virginia Company, raising
more than 29,000 pounds sterling before they ended in
1621. Recruiting laborers willing to settle and work in
Virginia, and obtaining supplies for them, were other
challenges. The Virginia Company promised food,
clothes, tools, housing and transportation to Virginia,
all at Company expense. However, supplies for the
colonists, bought in London and surrounding areas, often were insufficient or of poor quality. The laborers
had to work for the Company for up to seven years, and
then they would be released from service, with the possibility of acquiring their own land. The Company tried
to maintain its colony by obtaining several new char-
ters from King James I that reflected changes that its
management was making to more efficiently run the
colony. It also continued to work on raising funds and
recruiting people to go to Virginia. But the costs were
always high. Selling stock and running lotteries could
not keep the Company out of debt. When no profit was
raised to pay those who had bought stock, the Company
gave them land in Virginia. In England, the Company
went through a number of reorganizations. In 1618 a new
treasurer came to power, Sir Edwin Sandys. In the next
few years the leadership argued over the proper focus

for the colony. Bankruptcy and mismanagement of funds by Company leaders took their toll. Fewer people were willing to go to Virginia after a devastating war with the Powhatan Indians in 1622. At that point, King James I sent commissioners to investigate the Company and the colony and decided to revoke the Company's charter. In 1624 Virginia became a royal colony, answerable to the monarch's privy council.

OTHER SOURCES

Barbour, Philip, ed. The Jamestown Voyages Under the First Charter, 1606-1609. Cambridge University Press, 1969.

Billings, Warren. Jamestown and the Founding of the Nation. Gettysburg: Thomas Publications, 1991.

Craven, Wesley Frank. Dissolution of the Virginia Company. Gloucester, MA: Peter Smith, 1964.

Craven, Wesley Frank. The Virginia Company of London, 1606-1624. Williamsburg, VA: Virginia 350th Anniversary Celebration Corporation, 1957.

Rabb, Theodore. Enterprise and Empire: Merchant and Gentry Investment in the Expansion of England, 1575-1630. Cambridge, MA: Harvard University Press, 1967.

Historical background materials made possible by Archibald Andrews Marks.

The Virginia Company of London was raking in the loot. They had the Virginia colonies sewed up. The colonies in general had become quite lucrative for England and all companies involved. Ben Franklin, Thomas Jefferson, the French, and others as you will see, wanted a cut of the action. They could not get it, so they plotted up on a regime change. The plan was to usurp the English, run them out, take over all of their companies and cut deals with the companies with whom they could...those companies "too big to fail." America represented too much wealth for the English to have it all, at least that's what Washington, Franklin, Jefferson and Co. thought. This was the mid 1700s, and in fact, Franklin had started his campaign of propaganda by printing seditionist cartoons and articles as early as May 9th 1754, when he published what I believed to be the first political cartoon of a chopped up snake with the caption, "Join of Die," in which he was yeasting up the British colonies to unite against French incursions in the western interior. He was buddy's with France, why would he do that? You figure it out. The actual supposed "revolution" did not take place until the 1770s, so you can see the plan for regime change had started awhile back, and Franklin being in the printing business since the 1730s, he knew the full value of propaganda in print. Long story short, there was a work up towards the "revolution" and during this work up there had to be a corporate construct ready to immediately put in place once the British were expelled from the colonies. There had to be a populace primed and ready to go, and there had to be first and foremost "outside validation from a world nation" in order for the "revolution" to be swallowed by the outside world as legit. George Washington would help with that part. George Washington would enlist the help of another conspirator, the Sultan of Morocco. Going back to the history of the Moors, they were once a great power, they were deposed by Spain in the 1490's and last marched out in 1610. The Sultan of Morocco had world standing, and the usurpation of Britain in America could once again establish the Moors as a major world player. George Washington and Franklin knew this. They knew that Morocco could offer the legitimacy that the new break away republic would need to have world standing and they knew the "numbers were right" in terms of the project being doable. They just had to convince the Sultan of Morocco to get onboard. In fact they did, and prior to the actual constitution being instituted, it would first be sent to the Sultan of Morocco for his approval. What? Huh? Washington, the father of the country, sought counsel and approval from a Muslim Ruler, a slaver, for his enterprise in the colonies. From George Washington to Sidi Mohammed:

"1 December 1789 To Sidi Mohammed, Since the Date of the Letter, which the late Congress, by their President, addressed to your Imperial Majesty, the United States of America have thought proper to change their Government, and to institute a new one, agreeable to the Constitution, of which I have the Honor of, herewith, enclosing a Copy. The Time necessarily employed in this arduous Task, and the Derangements occasioned by so great, though peaceable a Revolution, will apologize, and account for your Majesty's not having received those regular Advices, and Marks of Attention, from the United States, which the Friendship and Magnanimity of your Conduct, towards them, afforded Reason to expect. The United States, having unanimously appointed me to the supreme executive Authority, in this Nation, your Majesty's Letter of the 17th August 1788, which, by Reason of the Dissolution of the late Government, remained unanswered, has been delivered to me. I have also received the Letters which your Imperial Majesty has been so kind as to write, in Favor of the United States, to the Bashaws of Tunis and Tripoli, and I present to you the sincere acknowledgments, and Thanks of the United States, for this important Mark of your Friendship for them. We greatly regret that the hostile Disposition of those Regencies, towards this Nation, who have never injured them, is not to be removed, on Terms in our Power to comply with. Within our Territories there are no Mines, either of Gold, or Silver, and this young Nation, just recovering from the Waste and Desolation of a long War, have not, as yet, had Time to acquire Riches by Agriculture and Commerce. But our Soil is bountiful, and our People industrious; and we have Reason to flatter ourselves, that we shall gradually become useful to our Friends. The Encouragement which your Majesty has been pleased, generously,

to give to our Commerce with your Dominions; the Punc-
tuality with which you have caused the Treaty with us
to be observed, and the just and generous Measures tak-
en, in the Case of Captain Proctor, made a deep Impres-
sion on the United States, and confirm their Respect
for, and Attachment to your Imperial Majesty. It gives
me Pleasure to have this Opportunity of assuring your
Majesty that, while I remain at the Head of this Nation, I shall not cease to promote every Measure that
may conduce to the Friendship and Harmony, which so
happily subsist between your Empire and them, and shall
esteem myself happy in every Occasion of convincing
your Majesty of the high Sense (which in common with
the whole Nation) I entertain of the Magnanimity, Wis-
dom, and Benevolence of your Majesty. In the Course of
the approaching Winter, the national Legislature (which
is called by the former Name of Congress) will assem-
ble, and I shall take Care that Nothing be omitted that
may be necessary to cause the Correspondence, between
our Countries, to be maintained and conducted in a Manner agreeable to your Majesty, and satisfactory to all
the Parties concerned in it. May the Almighty bless
your Imperial Majesty, our great and magnanimous
Friend, with his constant Guidance and Protection.
Written at the City of New York the first Day of December 1789. https://founders.archives.gov/documents/Wash-
ington/05-04-02-0251

With that letter it was a done deal. Morocco would be
the first world nation to recognize the United States
as a country, followed closely by France. The U.S.
Treaty of Peace and Friendship with Morocco is the oldest and longest lasting treaty in the U.S. On a side
note, the Emperor of Morocco, Moulay Ismael, "The
Bloodthirsty" enslaved 20,000 White people from Europe
and the British Isles to build his palace at Meknes and
ran an absolute iron fisted regime until his death in

1727.

"Sultan Moulay Ismail Ibn Sharif was propelled to the throne of Morocco in 1672. His brother had been riding horseback after a victory banquet and was killed when his horse galloped beneath the low-hanging branches of the palace orchard.

Ismail's reign as sultan, from 1672-1727, was longer than any other ruler in Moroccan history. Whether he should be remembered more for his beautiful creations or his cruel tyranny is a matter of dispute — but everyone agrees that Ismail was one of the most important rulers in Moroccan history.

Ismail was not, by any accounts, a very nice man. In fact, he's been quoted as having said, "My subjects are like rats in a basket, and if I do not keep shaking the basket, they will gnaw their way through."

It's estimated that 30,000 poor souls met their deaths at the hands of the sultan — often for no reason. He was well known to kill people during fits of rage. According to one story, the sultan lopped off the head of a slave who had been adjusting his stirrup as he was mounting his horse. They didn't call him "the Blood-thirsty" for nothing. Ismail was well-known for siring hundreds of children. According to the *Guinness Book of World Records*, he fathered 888 children — the highest number of offspring for anyone throughout history that can be verified. He was fiercely protective of his four wives and 500 concubines. Whenever a tribe surrendered to Moulay Ismail, the leader was forced to offer his most beautiful daughter to the sultan as a gift.

The women were treated like Ismail's favorite toys. Each concubine was granted a personal eunuch, a castrated male slave, and an odalisque, or female attendant. The lake-like Bassin de l'Agdal in Meknès served as an emergency source of water in times of war and a pool for his concubines in times of peace.

Men who merely glanced at one of his wives or concubines were punished by death. It's said that men who encountered the sultan's women laid facing the ground, so as to avoid any accusation of having looked upon them. If any of Ismail's harem were suspected of adultery, they were severely punished or put to death. The women were either strangled by the sultan himself or had their breasts cut off or teeth extracted. Ismail succeeded the throne at the age of 26 and established Meknès as the capital of the kingdom. He was a member of the Sharif dynasty, which claimed to be descendants of the Prophet Mohammed, the founder of Islam. Ismail used this pretense to justify his actions, both cruel and kind. His subjects bowed in his presence, and were not allowed to look him in the eye. During his 55-year reign, he managed to create magnificent and enormous construction projects. His palace was built exclusively by European slaves, aided by bands of local criminals. The palace was four miles in circumference, and its walls were 25 feet thick. As soon as he finished one project, he'd start on another. If he didn't like something, he would order it demolished and a new one rebuilt.

Ismail's favorite wife and queen of the palace was a black woman who started out as a concubine. Her name was Lalla Aisha Mubarka, or Zaydana, the name she acquired after giving birth to the sultan's first son, Zaydan. She held sway over Ismail and hatched a scheme to depose his favorite son, Mohammed al-Alim, suggesting that he intended to proclaim himself the sultan of

Morocco. For his punishment, Ismail had his son's left arm and right leg amputated for supposedly having rebelled against him. This was intended to send a message that any disobedience would mean severe punishment or death. Not surprisingly, Al-Alim died from blood loss. The formidable Black Guard was comprised of slave warriors acquired from sub-Saharan Africa. Considered loyal, as they no longer had any tribal affiliation, the Black Guard were Ismail's personal guards and servants. By the end of his reign, he had raised a powerful army of more than 150,000 men. These men had families and lived in communities of their own, but essentially belonged to Ismail. The boys were raised to serve in his army, which helped Ismail maintain his position and conquer the whole of Morocco from European kingdoms. The girls would marry, have children and continue the cycle.

The Black Guard exists to this day, though its name was changed to the Moroccan Royal Guard after the country gained its independence in 1956. The Habs Qara (Prison of Christian Slaves) was a large subterranean prison beneath the city of Meknès. At its height, it held an estimated 60,000 prisoners, 40,000 of them believed to have been Christian sailors captured at sea by Barbary pirates. The Christians were used as slave labor to build the city during the day and were shackled to the prison walls in the evening and forced to sleep standing up. Rumors of the existence of secret tunnels leading from the royal palace to the prison persist, despite lack of evidence. Ismail, the second ruler of the Alaouite dynasty, presided over Morocco at the same time that Louis XIV, the Sun King, ruled France. He and Louis XIV were close allies, and in 1682, Ismail sent Mohammed Tenim, the governor of Tétouan, to be his ambassador in France to sign a treaty of friendship and negotiate the release of Moroccan captives. French

Baroque painter Charles Antoine Coypel depicted the Moroccan ambassador's visit in his painting titled *Mohammed Tenim, Ambassadeur du Maroc à la Comédie Italienne*. Ismail sent his ambassador with a marriage proposal to Marie Anne de Bourbon, the eldest legitimized daughter of the king and his mistress Louise de La Vallière, but she declined. Thankfully, it didn't lead to an international incident."

http://www.thenotsoinnocentsabroad.com/blog/8-frightening-facts-about-sultan-moulay-ismail-ibn-sharif

"The end of Moulay Ismail's reign was marked by military setbacks and family problems relating to the succession. In May 1692, Moulay Ismail sent his son Moulay Zeydan with a large army to attack Ottoman Algeria. He was defeated by the Ottomans who counter-attacked and advanced as far as the Moulouya River. Ismail was forced to send an embassy to Algiers to make peace. In 1693, Moulay Ismail raided the Oran region and attempted to pillage the Beni Amer. The city of Oran resisted two attacks, forcing the sultan to beat a retreat. This time, it was the Turks who sent envoys to make peace, at the initiative of the Ottoman Sultan, Ahmed II. Ismail attempted to besiege the city of Ceuta with an army of 40,000 soldiers, but the strength of Spanish resistance meant that the siege went on and on. Part of Ismail's army also besieged Melilla from 1694 to 1696, but the city's fortifications were too much for them.

In spring 1701, Moulay Ismail launched another expedition against Algeria. The Moroccan forces advanced to the Chelif River before they were intercepted by the Ottoman army in Chedbiouïa. With a force of 10,000-12,000 men, the Algerian army managed to defeat the 60,000 soldiers of the Moroccan army. The Moroccan army suffered a heavy defeated and fell into disarray.

58

Moulay Ismail himself was wounded and barely escaped. The heads of 3,000 Moroccan soldiers and 50 Moroccan leaders were brought to Algiers. In 1702, Moulay Ismail gave his son Moulay Zeydan an army of 12,000 men and instructed him to capture the Peñón de Vélez de la Gomera. The Moroccans razed the Spanish fortress, but failed to retain la Isleta. Meanwhile, the English admiral, George Rooke joined in the siege of Ceuta, blockading the port in 1704. Between 1699 and 1700, Moulay Ismail divided the provinces of Morocco between his children. Moulay Ahmed was given responsibility for the province of Tadla and a force of 3,000 Black Guards. Moulay Abdalmalik was entrusted with Draâ province, with a kasbah and 1,000 cavalry. Moulay Mohammed al-Alam received Souss and 3,000 cavalry. Moulay El-Mâmoun commanded Sijilmassa and received 500 cavalry. When he died, he was replaced two years later by Moulay Youssef. Moulay Zeydan received to command of Cherg, but he lost it after the Ottomans attacked and Ismail made peace with them. He was then replaced by Moulay Hafid. This division of the realm provoked jealousy and rivalry between Ismail's sons, which sometimes degenerated into open clashes. In one of these, Moulay Abdelmalek was defeated by his brother, Moulay Nasser, who took control of the whole of Draâ. Moulay Sharif was appointed governor of Draâ by his father in place of Abdelmalek and succeeded in retaking the region from Nasser. In response to the intrigues, slanders and opposition of Lalla Aisha Mubarka, who wanted her son Moulay Zeydan to succeed his father as Sultan, Ismail's eldest son Moulay Mohammed al-Alam revolted in Souss and took control of Marrakesh on 9 March 1703. When Moulay Zeydan arrived with an army, Mohammed al-Alam fled to Taroudant. His brother besieged the place and captured it on 25 June 1704, and took him to Oued Beht on 7 July. Mohammed al-Alam was harshly punished by his father, who amputated one hand and one arm, executing both the butcher who refused to spill Mohammed al-

Alam's blood on the grounds that he was a Sharif, and the one who agreed to do it. He subsequently eliminated a caid of Marrakesh who had been responsible for Moulay Mohammed al-Alam's acquisition of the city, with exceptional violence. Moulay al-Alam committed suicide at Meknes on 18 July, despite precautions that his father had put in place to prevent this. On learning of the atrocities which Moulay Zeydan had committed at Taroudant, especially the massacre of the city's inhabitants, Moulay Ismail organised for him to be murdered in 1707, having his wives smother him when he was black-out drunk. Moulay Nasser also revolted in Souss, but was eventually killed by the Oulad Delim, who remained loyal to Moulay Ismail. To prevent further trouble, Moulay Ismail rescinded the governorships that he had conferred on his sons, except for Moulay Ahmed, who retained his post as governor of Tadla and Moulay Abdelmalek who became governor of Souss. Since Abdelmalek behaved like an independent and absolute monarch and refused to pay tribute, Ismail decided to change the order of succession - this was aided by the fact that Abdelmalek's mother was no longer close to him. Abdelmalek belatedly apologies, but Ismail remained hostile to his son. As a result, Moulay Ismail chose Moulay Ahmed as his successor. In 1720, Philip V of Spain, who wanted to get revenge on Morocco for having aided the Grand Alliance in the War of the Spanish Succession, sent a fleet commanded by the Marquess of Lede to raise the siege of Ceuta which had been ongoing since 1694 and to force the Moroccans to give up on retaking the city. The Spanish fleet managed to raise the siege, but Moulay Ismail resumed it in 1721, after the Marquess of Lede had returned to Spain. The Sultan further planned a large armada for an invasion of Spain, but it was destroyed by a storm in 1722. The siege of Ceuta continued until Ismail's death in 1727. Moulay Ismail ibn Sharif finally died on 22 March 1727 at the age of 81, from an abcess in his lower abdomen. His reign had lasted 57 years. He was succeeded by Moulay Ahmed. The empire immediately fell into civil war, as a result of a rebellion of the Black Guards. More than seven claimants to the throne succeeded to power between 1727 and 1757, some of them repeatedly, like Moulay Abdallah who was Sultan six times.

http://www.wikiwand.com/en/Ismail_Ibn_Sharif

So there it is. The U.S. is founded on regime change and collusion with an "African" Muslim nation of merchants and slavers. All of the fluff and puff about "patriotism" and heroics is just for the silly people. George Washington was a slaver himself. The "founding fathers" and European interests had thrown in with what was left of the Moroccan Empire, who was desperate to regain its glory, and decided to basically run the British out and hijack for whatever was left. It was a bold proposition and it required bold "blood thirsty" conspirators. Besides, the Moor's, Estevanico from Azemmour, Morocco, had been across North America in 1536, had discovered Arizona and New Mexico in 1539.

"Lastly the "negro," Estevanico was an Arab Moor, from the town of Azamor, on the Atlantic coast of Morocco...

THE JOURNEY OF Alvar Nunez Cabeza deVaca And HIS COMPANIONS from Florida to the Pacific 1528-1536 Copyright, 1904, by Williams'Barker Co.

The Moors knew exactly what revenue could be generated in North America. This is why they were "chomping at the bit" to recognize the new project United States. All parties involved took it as a "given" that slavery would be part of the project, in fact, as slaves were currency, I dont actually believe that the issue of slavery was even a cognizable issue to most. Almost like today, people dont question the currency, they just spend it. It was no secret that part and parcel with the new project would be agriculture, ranching, mining, everything else, and slaves, what else you wanna know? Keep in mind that it was also a given that those "slaves" would mean anybody, any color, from any where.

Now one can come to understand why White folks were being trafficked right along with 'Black Indians,' Copper Indians, Mexicans and Africans. It was business and no one saw any wrong in it. In fact George Washington, a slaver, wrote to "Captain Joh Thompson from Mt. Vernon, July 2 1776:

Sir: With this letter comes a negro, (Tom) which I beg the favor of you to sell in any of the islands you may go on for whatever he will fetch and bring me in return from him:

One had. Molasses, One ditto of best rum etc., etc."

The writings of George Washington, Vol ii. p. 211 N.Y. 1889, J.A. Rodgers, 100 Amazing facts about the Negro, p.26. Wesleyan University Press 1995

So now we can see in action, Washington utilizing a slave as currency and sending black slaves "out of America" abroad. This was the plan. With the help of the Moors, there would be a ready supply of aboriginals in America for labor and export. In fact, Franklin in his writing expressed his desire to rid the North American land of the "savages"(Lincoln, as well). That plan was put in motion and the operation commenced, and just like any big organized business, there is ALWAYS going to be "small time operators" who want to get in on the action. It was the small time ruthless operators who viewed anyone as currency. If you happened to be White, oh well, you got dipped in dye, raped, sedated or beat and off to the slave block with the niggers. All legal. This is the foundation for slavery of everyone in America, slavery was the economic engine that powered the world. Slavery was the way of the world and the international players, and local players in the "revolution" were all partakers of the practice. Lastly on Washington, the so called, "Father of the Country." The right wing nutty patriots would have everyone believe that Washington was some sort of deity, and certain news organizations spew out all manners of hate for Islamic people world wide, when in all honesty there would be no United States if not for the support of the Sultan of Morocco. It was a Sultan that Washington consulted and sought approval from first before he made any moves in North America. There also would not have been a "revolution" or United States if it wasn't for Phoebe Fraunces, daughter of "Black Sam" Fraunces, a "negro free" woman who in 1776 warned Washington of some poisoned peas that he was about to eat. The peas were poisoned by Washington's bodyguard, Thomas Hickey, an Irishman, who was hanged in New York City in front of a crown of 20,000. The world was a very different and complex world than the one people have been led to believe it was. The world was multi cultured, full of international corporate machinations, and the ultra high velocity of economics became a runaway train, and still is.

People are fodder, bottom line. My issue is how the textbooks twist facts, omit facts and create a false reality in the minds of children, who grow up into adults, and act upon that false reality. Those who act upon that falsehood, treat others like shit, act as if they have some sort of entitlement, and yell out of truck windows, "Go back to Africa nigger." Those who act upon the falsehood with their heads down, feeling sorry for themselves, no self pride, hating everybody, and why? Because some teacher told them some bullshit as a child, they grew up believing it, and now as adults, they act upon it by existing as such? It's a cold brainwashing, and tax dollars pay for it. Qui bono? Who benefits? You figure it out. The strange part of the foolishness is this, "the teachers" dont even know they are being bullshitted as well. They have that glazed kooky look in their eyes while they spew and parrot fairytales to White and Black children, all the while creating generations of mental illness. That's another story. Again, the "go back to Africa" mantra actually started with Franklin. He wanted to cleanse North America of all the aboriginal "swarthy" inhabitants and install the "red" or Mongol/Siberian natives in their steed, as in the Dawes Rolls of later history whereby Whites paid 5.00 to be declared "Indians," and given land, which is why so many so called "Indians" are now so white in hue.

"Which leads me to add one Remark: That the Number of purely white People in the World is proportionally very small. All Africa is black or tawny. Asia chiefly tawny. America (exlusive of the New Comers) wholly so. And in Europe, the Spaniards, Italians, French, Russians and Swedes, are generally of what we call a swarthy Complexion; as are the Germans also, the Saxons only excepted, who with the English, make the principal Body of White People on the Face of the Earth. I could wish their Numbers were increased. And while we are, as I may call it, Scouring our Planet, by clearing America of Woods, and so making this Side of our Globe reflect a brighter Light to the Eyes of Inhabitants in Mars or Venus (huh?), why should we in the Sight of Superior Beings, darken its People? why increase the Sons of Africa, by Planting them in America, where we have so fair an Opportunity, by excluding all Blacks and Tawneys, of increasing the lovely White and Red? But perhaps I am partial to the Complexion of my Country, for such Kind of Partiality is natural to Mankind. " Benjamin Franklin, "Observations Concerning the Increase of Mankind, Peopling of Countries, &c." (1751)

Documents in United States History- pp.129
Prentice Hall, Upper Saddle River, New Jerey 07458

Besides Franklin's Mars or Venus gibberish, the entire
spiel is basically the same 'ole same 'ole, " make as
much loot as possible" we are entitled to it, and crush
anyone who gets in the way. Also, as with Washington,
Jefferson, Lincoln, inter alia, Thomas Paine, James
Adams, James Madison, and Napoleon, they were all open
believers in the practice of Deism. In a nutshell, from
the mouth of Thomas Paine we hear:

"I do not believe in the creed professed by the Jewish
church, by the Roman church, by the Greek church, by
the Turkish church, by the Protestant church, nor by
any church that I know of. My own mind is my own
church. All national institutions of churches, whether
Jewish, Christian or Turkish, appear to me no other
than human inventions, set up to terrify and enslave
mankind, and monopolize power and profit. Each of those
churches show certain books, which they call revela-
tion, or the word of God. The Jews say, that their word
of God was given by God to Moses, face to face; the
Christians say, that their word of God came by divine
inspiration: and the Turks say, that their word of God
(the Koran) was brought by an angel from Heaven. Each
of those churches accuse the other of unbelief; and for
my own part, I disbelieve them all. It is curious to
observe how the theory of what is called the Christian
church sprung out of the tail of the heathen mythology.
A direct incorporation took place in the first instance, by making the reputed founder to be celestially
begotten. The trinity of gods that then followed was no
other than a reduction of the former plurality, which
was about twenty or thirty thousand: the statue of Mary
succeeded the statue of Diana of Ephesus; the deifica-
tion of heroes changed into the canonization of saints;
the Mythologists had gods for everything; the Christian

65

Mythologists had saints for everything; the church became as crowded with one, as the Pantheon had been with the other, and Rome was the place of both. The Christian theory is little else than the idolatry of the ancient Mythologists, accommodated to the purposes of power and revenue; and it yet remains to reason and philosophy to abolish the amphibious fraud. "
The Age of Reason, Thomas Paine, 1794.

This was the thinking of the Deist. They believed "God" existed, however "logic" and "reason" were now deity and therefore whatever could be seen as "reasonable" was cool. It was reasonable, in their eyes, to loot an pillage an entire continent while masquerading as some benevolent cause. It was logical, they felt, to earn money, by any means necessary, and set up a structure of perpetual revenue that functions to this day. People are fodder. The United States project was the only thing in the minds of Washington, The Sultan of Morocco, and the "Founding Fathers." It just so happened that slavery would have to play a role in it, and White folks would be slaves too. That part of history has somehow been omitted. Besides, it doesn't fit the narrative, you know, "White people chattel slaves in all." That would be too real. Gradually, over the generations, through the use of compulsory education, Whites would, like the layers of an onion, peel off their nigger persona, to become the people they are today. White people came to America, started calling copper colored people niggers, all the while a few generations back, they were niggers too. The pot calling the kettle black, literally.

"The evidence makes it clear that the first Europeans were dark skinned. Olalde et al.(2014) provides conclusive genetic evidence that hunter gatherers in Mesolithic Europe were dark skinned or highly pigmented with light (blue) eyes. The Olalde et al.(2014)

study of La Brana-Arintero site in Leon, Spain of dark skinned hunter-gatherer Europeans corresponds to the Loschbour sample from Luxembourg, of dark skinned Europeans. This cline of pigmentation in western Eurasia appears to be associated with Cro-Magnon man, the first AMH in western Europe who was associated with the Aurignacian culture. The first AMH European reconstructed byForensic artist Richard Neave, of National Geographic from 35 kya resembled a Khoisan individual. This supports the research of Boule and Vallois (1957) that South Africans migrated across Africa, into Europe over 35 kya. Most researchers maintain that the first AMH European came from the Levant. This migration of AMH entering western Eurasia from the East is not supported by the archaeological evidence. The Auriganacian culture which is associated with the Cro-Magnon people crossed the Straits of Gibraltar (SG) from Africa into Iberia. (Winters, 2008, 2011). We know that the first AMH probably entered western Eurasia via the SG, because Neanderthals dominated the Levant until around 30- 20 kya. Between 10- 5 kya the Levant population was "tropically adapted" hominids, especially in relation to Qafzed-Skhul (QS) hominids (Holliday, 2000). Ninety-five percent of the QS population were SSA (e.g., Qafzeh 8 at 85%, and Skhul 4 at 71%)(Holliday, 2000). The fauna and zooarchaeological remains from QS, indicate the hominids here exploited African fauna (Holliday, 2000). Holliday (2000) claims the QS people were Proto-Cro-Magnons, because they were similar in dental and craniological size to the Aurignacian hominids(Holliday, 2000). Except of the AMH at QS, the majority of hominids in the Levant were Neanderthal. The craniometric evidence for SSA populations in Europe was also examined by Brace et al. (2006). Brace et al. (2006) after studying 24 craniofacial measurements of AMH from Europe was surprised to find that Neolithic people in Europe fail to be related to modern Europeans. Some researchers have assumed that the Basque, a non-Indo-European population in Spain probably represented descendants of the original Europeans, but samples from this group and Canary Islanders did not correspond to the Natufians or Cro-Magnon populations (Brace, 2006). The founders of civilization in Southwest Asia were the people, archaeologists call Natufians. By 13,000 BC, according to Clark(1977) the Natufians were collecting grasses in Nubia (Ehret, 1979), which later became domesticated crops in Southwest Asia. In Palestine the Natufians established intensive grass collection. The Natfians used the Ibero-Maurusian tool industry (Wendorf, 1968). The Aurignacian civilization was founded by the Cro-Magnon people who originated in Iberia. They took this culture to Western Europe across the Straits of Gibraltar (Winters, 2011). The Cro-Magnon people were probably Bushman/Khoisan (Boule & Vallois, 1957). The "Classic Aurignacian" culture probably began in Africa, crossed the Straits of Gibraltar into Iberia, and expanded eastward across Europe (Brown, 2006; Gilead, 2005; Steven et al. , 2001; Winters, 2008, 2011). The archaeological record informs us that Cro-Magnon people replaced the Neanderthal population of the Levant, at Ksar Akil around 32,000 years ago (Steven et al., 2001; Gilead,2005), not the Natufians who entered the Levant almost 20,000 years later. This indicates that the Aurignacians moved west to east from Iberia across Europe. The archaeological and craniometric evidence indicates that the preIndo-European people were probably highly pigmented. There have been numerous "Negroid skeletons" found in Europe according to Boule and Vallois (1957). Diop (1991) discussed the Negroes of Europe in Civilization or Barbarism (pp. 25-68). Also Boule and Vallois (1957) reported the find of SSA skeletons at, Grotte des Enfants, Chamblandes in Switzerland, several Ligurian and Lombard tombs of the Metal Ages have also yielded evidences of a Negroid element. Since the publication of Verneau's memoir, discoveries of other Negroid skeletons in Neolithic levels in Illyria and the Balkans have been announced. The prehistoric statues, dating from the Copper Age, from Sultan Selo in Bulgaria are also thought to protray Negroids (Boule & Vallois, 1957). In 1928 Rene Bailly found in one of the caverns of Moniat, near Dinant in Belgium, a human skeleton of whose age it is difficult to be certain, but seems definitely prehistoric. It is remarkable for its Negroid characters, which give it a reseblance to the skeletons from both Grimaldi and Asselar (Diop, 1991). Boule and Vallois (1957), was able to chart the migration of civilization from South Africa to the Aurignacian culture of Europe. These anthropologist reported that the Khoisan shared the same style stone implements and burials "associated with the Aurignacian or Solutrean type industry..."(Boule & Vallois, 1957: pp. 318-319). They add, that in relation to Bushman [Khoisan] art "This almost uninterrupted series leads us to regard the African continent as a centre of importantmigrations which at certain times may have played a great part in the stocking of Southern Europe. Finally, we must not forget that the Grimaldi Negroid skeletons show many points of resemblance with the Bushman [Khoisan] skeletons" (Boule & Vallois, 1957) In conclusion, the ancient Europeans were dark skinned. They carried mtDNA haplogroups H, N, and U, and probably y-chromosomes A and C6. Some of these Blacks had blue eyes. These Black Europeans carried haplogroups H and N. These haplogroups continue to be carried by Sub Saharan African. This is based on the reality that the haplogroup N1(a) is common to Senegambians, modern Ethiopians and the Dravidian speaking people of India; and the craniometric evidence indicated that the Aurignacian and Neolithic populations were Sub-Saharan Africans(Boule & Vallois, 1957; Diop,1991). Thus, the ancient hunter-gather Europeans and European farmers were related to African groups. These dark skinned people probably planted the seeds of agriculture in ancient Europe.Interestingly, between 23,000-7000 BC the dominant haplogroup of Western Eurasians remained hg N1."

Advances in Anthropology , 2014, 4, 124-132 Published Online August 2014 in SciRes.   http://www.scir-p.org/journal/aa
http://dx.doi.org/10.4236/aa.2014.43016

WHITE PEOPLES IMAGINATION-

Deep down inside, White folks always have a fear of
Black people. Its been drilled into them since birth.
They have been so fully brainwashed by the media,
movies and educational system, until they actually
function out of a position of fear on a daily basis.
Fear of illness, fear of crime, fear of political parties, fear of immigrants, fear of outer space, fear of
enlightenment, and you name it. Pick a fear. The social engineers love fear. Fear makes people do things
they would not logically or reasonably do otherwise.
Lets go back to some old school fear mongering.....

NAT TURNER REBELLION?

Classic fear propaganda. There was no T.V. or internet
so the only game in town was print media. It was print
media that pushed forward the false notion of a "slave
rebellion." This story has all the 'trimmings' for a
good scary fear mongering fairy tale, to wit, "A mob of
salivating slave niggers on a rampage, burning up everything, raping White women, and hacking up White
men."

That's the pinnacle of White fear. The media still
keeps this image going with movies like "Chaka Zulu"
and news stories featuring packs of Africans wielding
machetes whenever they want to scare the viewing audi-
ence, or "Black Friday" mobs fighting over T.V. set-
s.The Nat Turner story is bullshit. This story was concocted to instill fear in populace, White and Black
alike, and as usual this false propaganda created real
circumstances:

"A reign of terror followed in Virginia. Labor was
paralyzed, plantations abandoned, women and children

were driven from home and crowded into nooks and corners. The sufferings of many of these refugees who spent night after night in the woods were intense. Retaliation began. In a little more than one day 120 Negroes were killed. The newspapers of the times contained from day to day indignant protests against the cruelties perpetrated.

One individual boasted that he himself had killed between ten and fifteen Negroes. Volunteer whites rode in all directions visiting plantations. Negroes were tortured to death, burned, maimed and subjected to nameless atrocities. Slaves who were distrusted were pointed out and if they endeavored to escape, they were ruthlessly shot down."A few individual instances will show the nature and extent of this vengeance. "A party of horsemen started from Richmond with the intention of killing every colored person they saw in Southampton County. They stopped opposite the cabin of a free colored man who was hoeing in his little field. They called out, 'Is this Southampton County?' He replied, 'Yes Sir, you have just crossed the line, by yonder tree.' They shot him dead and rode on."A slaveholder went to the woods accompanied by a faithful slave, who had been the means of saving his master's life during the insurrection. When they reached a retired place in the forest, the man handed his gun to his master, informing him that he could not live a slave any longer, and requested either to free him or shoot him on the spot. The master took the gun in some trepidation, leveled it at the faithful Negro and shot him through the heart. But these outrages were not limited to the Negro population. There occurred other instances which strikingly remind one of scenes before the Civil War and during reconstruction. An Englishman, named Robinson, was engaged in selling books at Petersburg. An alarm being given one night that five hundred blacks were marching against the town, he stood guard with others at the bridge. After the panic had a little subsided he happened to make the remark that the blacks as men were entitled to their freedom and ought to be emancipated. This led to great excitement and the man was warned to leave the town. He took passage in the stage coach, but the vehicle was intercepted. He then fled to a friend's home but the house was broken open and he was dragged forth. The civil authorities informed of the affair refused to interfere. The mob stripped him, gave him a considerable number of lashes and sent him on foot naked under a hot sun to Richmond, whence he with difficulty found passage to New York."

"Believing that Nat Turner's insurrection was a general conspiracy, the people throughout the State were highly excited. The Governor of the commonwealth quickly called into service whatever forces were at his command. The lack of adequate munitions of war being apparent, Commodore Warrington, in command of the Navy Yard in Gosport, was induced to distribute a portion of the public arms under his control. For this purpose the government ordered detachments of the Light Infantry from the seventh and fifty-fourth Regiments and from the fourth Regiment of cavalry and also from the fourth Light Artillery to take the field under Brigadier General Eppes. Two regiments in Brunswick and Greenville were also called into service under General William H. Brodnax and continued in the field until the danger had passed. Further aid was afforded by Commodore Eliott of the United States Navy by order of whom a detachment of sailors from the Natchez was secured and assistance also from Colonel House, the commanding officer at Fortress Monroe, who promptly detacheda part of his force to take the field under Lieutenant Colonel Worth. The revolt was subdued, however, before these troops could be placed in action and about all they accomplished thereafter was the terrifying of Negroes who

had taken no part in the insurrection and the immola-
tion of others who were suspected. The news of the
Southampton insurrection thrilled the whole country,
North as well as South. The newspapers teemed with the
accounts of it.' Rumors of similar outbreaks prevailed
all over the State of Virginia and throughout the
South. There were rumors to the effect that Nat Turner
was everywhere at the same time. People returned home
before twilight, barricaded themselves in their homes,
kept watch during the night, or abandoned their homes
for centers where armed force was adequate to their
protection. There were many such false reports as the
one that two maid servants in Dinwiddie County had murdered an old lady and two children. Negroes throughout
the State were suspected, arrested and prosecuted on
the least pretext and in some cases murdered without
any cause. Almost any Negro having some of the much advertised characteristics of Nat Turner was in danger of
being run down and torn to pieces for Nat Turner himself. The excitement in other States was not much less
than in Virginia and North Carolina. In South Carolina
Governor Hayne issued a proclamation to quiet rumors of
similar uprisings. In Macon, Georgia, the entire population rose at midnight, roused from their beds by rumors of an impending onslaught. Slaves were arrested
and tied to trees in different parts of the State,
while captains of the militia delighted in hacking at
them with swords. In Alabama, rumors of a joint conspiracy of Indians and Negroes found ready credence. At
New Orleans the excitement was at such a height that a
report that 1,200 stands of arms were found in a black
man's house, was readily believed." But the people were
not satisfied with this flow of blood and passions were
not subdued with these public wreakings. Nat Turner was
still at large. He had eluded their constant vigilance
ever since the day of the raid in August."

Curiously enough, in this same account we read of some

sort of court proceedings that "supposedly" took place, however as of this writing, there does not exist ANY official court documents, case files, inter alia, abstract of judgment, execution order, or appellate filings. Nothing. No one has produced any evidence of the existence of Nat Turner except, newspaper reporters, authors and storytellers. Kinda like today....

"His arrest caused much relief. He was taken the next day to Jerusalem, the county seat, and tried on the fifth of November before a board of magistrates. The indictment against him was for making insurrection and plotting to take away the lives of divers free white persons on the twenty-second of August, 1831. On his arraignment Turner pleaded " Not Guilty. " The Commonwealth submitted its case, not on the testimony of any eye witnesses but on the depositions of one Levi Waller who read Turner's Confession' and Colonel Trezevant the committing magistrate corroborated it by referring to the same confession. Turner introduced no testimony in defense and his counsel made no argument in his behalf. He was promptly found guilty and sentenced to be hanged Friday, November 11, 1831, twelve days after his capture. Sidenote: Again, we are presented with the same notion-"deport the niggers." This is a reoccurring theme throughout American history. This also is the biggest support for the proposition that the African slave trade in America is a lie, and that in fact it was told in reverse. The slaves were been exported from America! That has always been the plan. At that time they needed an excuse to unite the White populace in this this plan and what better way to scare the people with some wild story? That way they could kill as many as they wanted, deport or remove them and create all types of legislation to facilitate such. That's what it was all about.

"Believing that the free people of color had been or

would be the most effective means in the attack on the
institution of slavery, there were more memorials for
the removal of this class of the population than any
other petitions bearing on slavery. Among the counties
praying for the removal of the free Negroes, were
Amelia, Isle of Wight, York, Nanosecond, Frederick,
Powhatan, Fair fax, and Cumberland. Others asked for
the removal of the free Negroes (aboriginal "Indians")
and furthermore the purchase of slaves to be deported.
Among the counties praying for such a measure were
Fauquier, Hanover, Washington, Nelson, Loudoun,
Prince William, and King William. From Charles City,
Rockbridge, and Caroline Counties came the additional
request for a legislation providing for gradual emancipation. Page, Augusta, Fauquier, and Botetourt, sent
memorials praying that steps be taken to procure an
amendment to the Constitution of the United States, in-
vesting Congress with the power to appropriate money
for sending beyond the limits of the United States the
free people of color and such of the slaves as might be
purchased for the same purpose. This was almost in
keeping with the request from the Henrico and Frederick
Colonization Societies asking the Government to deport
the Negroes to Africa. Buckingham County requested that
the colored population be removed from the county and
colonized according to the plans set forth by Thomas
Jefferson. The request of the Society of Friends in the
county of Charles City for gradual emancipation, however, caused resentment. Thinking that it might not be
possible to transport all the Negroes of the country
very easily, requests for dealing the the situation as
it was, were also in order. As a number of the farmers
had suffered from a loss of sheep by the numerous dogs
maintained by slaves and free persons of color, there
came requests praying that the keeping of dogs and hogs
by Negroes be made illegal. Some of these petitions,
too, had an economic phase. There came from Culpepper a
petition praying for a passage of the law for the en-

couragement of white mechanics by prohibiting any slave, free Negro or mulatto from being bound as an apprentice to learn any trade or art. Charles City and New Kent complained against the practice of employing slaves and Negroes as millers and asked that a law penalizing such action be enacted. The question as to what should be done with the blacks turned out to be the most important matter brought before the legislature. Three-fourths of the session was devoted to the discussion of such questions as the removal of the free Negroes and the colonization of such slaves as masters could be induced to give up. The legislature met on the 5th of December and after going through the preliminaries of organization listened to the message of the Governor which had the insurrection as its most prominent feature. When the petitions from the various counties began to come in, there soon prevailed a motion that so much of the Governor's message as related to the insurrection of slaves and the removal of the free Negroes be referred to a select committee, which after prolonged deliberation found it difficult to agree upon a report. Desiring to protect the interests of slavery, William O. Goode, of Mecklenburg County, moved on the eleventh of January that the select committee appointed to consider the memorials bearing on slaves free Negroes and the Southampton massacre be discharged from the consideration of all petitions, memorials and resolutions, which had for their object the manumission of slaves. The resolution further declared that it was not expedient to legislate on slavery. Whereupon Thomas Jefferson Randolph, of Albemarle County, moved to amend this resolution so as to instruct the committee to inquire into the expediency and to report a bill to submit to the voters of the State the propriety of providing by law that the children of all female slaves who might be born in that State on or after the fourth day of July, 1840, should become the property of the commonwealth, the males at the age of twenty-one years and females at the age of eighteen, if detained by their owners within the limits of the commonwealth, until they should respectively arrive at the ages aforesaid. They would then be hired out until the net sum arising therefrom should be sufficient to defray the expenses of their removal beyond the limits of the United States. The next effort of the legislature in dealing with the Negroes was to strengthen the black code as it then existed so as to provide for a more adequate supervision and rigid control of the slaves and free people of color (Aboriginal "Indians"). There was offered thereafter a bill to amend an act entitled "an act to revise under one the several acts concerning slaves, free Negroes and mulattoes." The important provisions of the bill were that slaves and free Negroes should not conduct religious exercises nor attend meetings held at night by white preachers unless granted written permission by their masters or overseers. Thereafter no free Negro should be capable of purchase or otherwise acquiring permanent ownership, except by descent, of any slave, other than his or her husband, wife or children. Further penalties, moreover, were provided for persons writing or printing anything intended to incite the Negroes to insurrection. The State had already enacted a law prohibiting the teaching of slaves, free Negroes and mulattoes. The other petitions requiring that Negroes be restricted in the higher pursuits of labor and in the ownership of hogs and dogs were, because of the spirit which existed after the excitement had subsided, rejected as unnecessary. The law providing for burning in the hand was repealed. The immigration of free Negroes into the State, however, was prohibited in 1834. The effect of this insurrection and this debate extended far beyond the borders of Virginia and the South. Governor McArthur of Ohio in a message to his legislature called special attention to the outbreak and the necessity for prohibitive legislation against the influx within that commonwealth of the free

people of color who naturally sought an asylum in the
free States. The effect in Southern States was far more
significant. Many of them already had sufficient regulations to meet such emergencies as that of an insurrection but others found it necessary to revise their
black codes. Maryland passed, at the session of its
legislature in 1831-1832, a law providing a board of
managers to use a fund appropriated for the purpose of
removing the free people of color to Liberia in connection with the State colonization society. Another act
forbade the introduction of slaves either for sale or
resident and the immigration of free Negroes. It imposed many disabilities on the resident free people of
color so as to force them to emigrate. Delaware, which
had by its constitution of 1831, restricted the
right of franchise to whites enacted in 1832 an act
preventing the use of firearms by free Negroes and provided also for the enforcement of the law of 1811
against the immigration of free Negroes and mulattoes,
prohibited meetings of blacks after ten o'clock and
forbade non-resident blacks to preach. In 1831 Tennessee forbade free persons of color to immigrate into
that State under the penalty of fine for remaining and
imprisonment in default of payment. Persons emancipat-
ing slaves had to give bond for their removal to some
point outside of the State and additional penalties
were provided for slaves found assembling or engaged in
conspiracy. Georgia enacted a measure to the effect
that none might give credit to free persons of color
without order from their guardian required by law and,
if insolvent, they might be bound out. It further provided that neither free Negroes nor slaves might preach
or exhort an assembly of more than seven unless licensed by justices on certificate of three ordained
ministers. They were also forbidden to carry firearms.
North Carolina, in which Negroes voted until 1834, enacted in 1831 a special law prohibiting free Negroes
from preaching and slaves from keeping house or going

at large as free men. To collect fines of free Negroes
the law authorized that they might be sold. The new
constitution of the State in 1835 restricted the right
of suffrage to white men. South Carolina passed in 1836
a law prohibiting the teaching of slaves to read and
write under penalties, forbidding too the employment of
a person of color as salesman in any house, store or
shop used for trading. Mississippi had already met most
of these requirements in the slave code in the year
1830. In Louisiana it was deemed necessary to strength-
en the slave code. An act relative to the introduction
of slaves provided that slaves should not be introduced
except by persons immigrating to reside and citizens
who might become owners.59 Previous legislation had already provided severe penalties for persons teaching
Negroes to read and write and also had made provision
for compelling free colored persons to leave the State.
In 1832 the State of Alabama enacted a law making it
unlawful for any free person of color to settle within
that commonwealth. Slaves or free persons of color
should not be taught to spell, read or write. It provided penalties for Negroes writing passes and for free
blacks associating or trading with slaves. More than
five male slaves were declared an unlawful assembly but
slaves could attend worship conducted by whites yet
neither slaves nor free Negroes were permitted to
preach unless before five respectable slaveholders and
the Negroes so preaching were to be licensed by some
neighboring religious society. It was provided, however, that these sections of the article did not apply to
or affect any free person of color who, by the treaty
between the United States and Spain, became citizens of
the United States."

The Aftermath of Nat Turner's Insurrection
Author(s): John W. Cromwell
Source: The Journal of Negro History,
Vol. 5, No. 2 (Apr., 1920), pp. 208-234

Published by: The University of Chicago Press on behalf of the Association for the Study of African American Life and History

That's why the fear must be maintained. The Whites must stay scared in order to maintain the ripe environment for the subjugation of an entire people, perpetually. It is apparent from the citations that not everyone Black was slave and the ones not slaves, it did not matter. The plan was to kill, deport or enslave ALL of the copper color people in America. Before moving on, I want to point out the complete arrogance of the corporate structure, please read this again:

"Like other southern states in the years leading up to 1857, Louisiana had taken legislative and judicial action to clarify the relationship of race and slavery. In the 1850s the legislature and courts of Louisiana tried to curb manumission, eliminate such states of "quasi-slavery" as infuturo emancipation, enforce a stricter segregation of social relations between black and white (especially drinking, gambling, and dancing), and regulate the public behavior of free people of color (Aboriginal "Indians") and slaves more vigilantly. By 1859 Louisiana would pass its own self-enslavement law and offer free people of color the chance to choose a master and enslave themselves." Who could even think of something such as that except a sick devil.

"The system of slavery demanded a special police force and such a force was made possible and unusually effective by the presence of the poor whites. This explains the difference between the slave revolts in the West Indies, and the lack of effective revolt in the Southern United States. In the West Indies, the power over the slave was held by the whites and carried out by them and such Negroes as they could trust. In the South, on the other hand, the great planters formed

proportionately quite as small a class but they had
singularly enough at their command some five million
poor whites; that is, there were actually more white
people to police the slaves than there were slaves.
Considering the economic rivalry of the black and white
worker in the North, it would have seemed natural that
the poor white would have refused to police the slaves.
But two considerations led him in the opposite direction. First of all, it gave him work and some authority
as overseer, slave driver, and member of the patrol
system. But above and beyond this, it fed his vanity
because it associated him with the masters.(He wasn't
master?) Slavery bred in the poor white a dislike of
Negro toil of all sorts. He never regarded himself as a
laborer, or as part of any labor movement. If he had
any ambition at all it was to become a planter and to
own "niggers." To these Negroes he transferred all the
dislike and hatred which he had for the whole slave
system. The result was that the system was held stable
and intact by the poor white. Even with the late ruin
of Haiti before their eyes, the planters, stirred as
they were, were nevertheless able to stamp out slave
revolt. The dozen revolts of the eighteenth century had
dwindled to the plot of Gabriel in 1800, of Vesey in
1822, of Nat Turner (fake) in 1831 and crews of the
Amistad and Creole in 1839 and 1841. Gradually the
whole white South became an armed and commissioned camp
to keep Negroes in slavery and to kill the black
rebel."
W.E.B. DuBois 1935, Black Reconstruction 1860-1880,
Harcourt Brace and Co.

BLACK SLAVE OWNERS

Earlier on in this book, we touched upon the fact that in some areas of America, Blacks owned so many White slaves that they had to pass a law against it. Black slave owners were very commonplace. In fact: "Having economic interests in common with the white slaveholders, the Negro owners of slaves often enjoyed the same social standing. It was not exceptional for them to attend the same church, to educate their children in the same private school, and to frequent the same places of amusement. Under such circumstances miscegenation easily followed. In the South where almost all of the Negro slaveholders were, moreover, we find some of them competing with the large planters in the number of slaves they owned. Most of such Negro proprietors lived in Louisiana, South Carolina, Maryland and Virginia, as did the majority of all such slave owners. There are, moreover, a few instances of confusing absentee ownership with Negro ownership. Sometimes a free Negro had charge of a plantation, but did not own the slaves himself, and the enumerator returned him as the owner. Excepting those of Louisiana, one may say that most of the Negro owners of slaves lived in urban communities. In those parts of the South where the influence of the kind planter near the coast was not felt, the Negro owner of slaves did not frequently appear. The free Negroes themselves, moreover, encountered such difficulties in the lower South and Southwest that they had to seek more hospitable communities in free States. By 1840 the trend toward degrading the free Negro to a lower status had become evident even in the apparently benevolent slave holding States. Just before the outbreak of the Civil War the free Negro was receiving practically no consideration in the South and very little in the North. History here repeats itself, then, in showing the varying attitude of the whites toward the blacks in the cycles of national development."

Free Negro Owners of Slaves in the United States in 1830 Compiled under the Direction of and edited by CARTER G. WOODSON Editor of The Journal of Negro History Copyright, 1924 By the Association for the Study of Negro Life and History, Inc.

This was the period when the press was on to start the degradation of Blacks in America, including, but not limited to, Aboriginal Indians, Free Persons of Color, Free Blacks and Mulatto's. These groups had to be suppressed for the White population to progress, and the suppression started at a base level, in primary education. This was the run up to the "civil war" and the aftermath known as "reconstruction." This was when the entire fake narrative began to take shape. That's why it is called "Reconstruction," because that what was done, an entire fairytale reconstruction that elevated Whites into a master class and everyone else into a slave. Straight up with no chaser. Anyone believing otherwise is a naive, silly, fool. The Journal of Negro History contains, literally, the names of hundreds of Black slave owners, listed by state and in alphabetical order. For the sake of brevity, I will not list each name, however the document is here:

https://ia800608.overarching/16/items/freenegroowner-so00wood/freenegroownerso00wood.pdf

My own family is listed there as well, as we have NEVER been slaves:

GUILLORY-

Alexandre 2 slaves	Bayou Touche	p. 48
Donatien L. 2 slaves	Bayou Têche	p. 51

84

Jean-Baptiste FPOC   Bayou Mallet   p. 30
18 slaves

Joseph   Bayou Têche   p. 46
2 slaves

Julien   Bayou Têche   p. 46
2 slaves

Lastie   Bayou Têche   p. 51
6 slaves

Leufroy   Grande-Prairie   p. 53
6 slaves

Pierre   Bayou Têche   p. 50
4 slaves

DONATO-

DONATTO Auguste   FPOC   Bayou Mallet   p. 30
4 slaves

Martin   FPOC Plaquemines-Brûlées p.12
75 slaves

1830 United States Federal Census, St. Landry's Parish
Slave Holder & Slave Statistics
Louis Andrus, Assistant Census Marshal
Prepared by CHRISTOPHE LANDRY

This just represents my family. Imagine all of the other families not recorded by the census. Slavery was not
as people are taught. Most slaves were in fact "contract employees" of the persons of color who owned
them, as well as extended family, as is the case with
my family. St. Landry's Parish alone had 631 Black
slave owners in 1830 that registered with the census.

It would be fair to say another 100 would go uncounted,
especially in areas that were "off limits" to all out-
siders, and there was many areas of Louisiana that out-
siders did not tread, census or not.

Slavery, again was not the way people are taught. There
was a White ruling class that didnt give a damn about
poor whites:

"It resolves itself into three classes,broadly distin-
guished from each other, and connected by no common interest — the slaves on whom devolves all the regular
industry, the slaveholders who reap all its fruits, and
an idle and lawless rabble who live dispersed over vast
plains in a condition little removed from absolute barbarism." From all that has been written and said about
the antebellum South, one almost loses sight of about
5,000,000 white people in i860 who lived in the South
and held no slaves. Even among the two million slaveholders, an oligarchy of 8,000 really ruled the
South,while as an observer said: "For twenty years, I
do not recollect ever to have seen or heard these
non-slaveholding whites referred to by the Southern
gentleman as constituting any part of what they called
the South." They were largely ignorant and degraded;
only 25% could read and write. The condition of the
poor whites has been many times described: "A wretched
log hut or two are the only habitations in sight. Her-
ereside, or rather take shelter, the miserable cultiva-
tors of the ground, or a still more destitute class who
make a precarious living by peddling 'lightwood' in the
city...."These cabins...are dens of filth. The bed if
there be a bed is a layer of something in the corner
that defies scenting. If the bed is nasty, what of the
floor? What of the whole enclosed space ? What of the
creatures themselves? Pough! Water in use as a purifier
is unknown. Their faces are bedaubed with the muddy accumulation of weeks. They just give them a wipe when

they see a stranger to take off the blackest dirt. The poor wretches seem startled when you address them, and answer your questions cowering like culprits."Olmsted said: "I saw as much close packing, filth and squalor, in certain blocks inhabited by laboring whites in Charleston, as I have witnessed in any Northern town of its size; and greater evidences of brutality and ruffianly character, than I have ever happened to see, among an equal population of this class, before." Two classes of poor whites have been differentiated: the mountain whites and the poor whites of the lowlands. "Below a dirty and ill-favored house, down under the bank on the shingle near the river, sits a family of five people, all ill-clothed and unclean; a blear-eyed old THE WHITEWORKER 27 woman, a younger woman with a mass of tangled red hair hanging about her shoulders, indubitably suckling a baby; a little girl with the same auburn evidence of Scotch ancestry; a boy, and a younger child all gathered about a fire made among some bricks, surrounding a couple of iron saucepans, in which is a dirty mixture looking like mud, but probably warmed-up sorghum syrup, which with a few pieces of corn pone, makes their breakfast. "Most of them are illiterate and more than correspondingly ignorant. Some of them had Indian ancestors and a few bear evidences of Negro blood. The so-called 'mountain boomer,' says an observer, 'has little self-respect and no self-reliance....So long as his corn pile lasts the "cracker" lives in contentment, feasting on a sort of hoe cake made of grated corn meal mixed with salt and water and baked before the hot coals, with addition of what game the forest furnishes him when he can get up the energy to go out and shoot or trap it.........The irregularities of their moral lives cause them no sense of shame....But, notwithstanding these low moral conceptions, they are of an intense religious excitability.' "Above this lowest mass rose a middle class of poor whites in the making. There were some small farmers who

had more than a mere sustenance and yet were not large planters. There were overseers. There was a growing class of merchants who traded with the slaves and free Negroes and became in many cases larger traders, dealing with the planters for the staple crops. Some poor whites rose to the professional class, so that the rift between the planters and the mass of the whites was partially bridged by this smaller intermediate class. While revolt against the domination of the planters over the poor whites was voiced by men like Helper, who called for a class struggle to destroy the planters, this was nullified by deep-rooted antagonism to the Negro, whether slave or free. If black labor could be expelled from the United States (SAME TOPIC AGAIN!) or eventually exterminated (DITTO), then the fight against the planter could take place. But the poor whites and their leaders could not for a moment contemplate a fight of united white and black labor against the exploiters. Indeed, the natural leaders of the poor whites, the small farmer, the merchant, the professional man, the white mechanic and slave overseer, were bound to the planters and repelled from the slaves and even from the mass of the white laborers in two ways: first, they constituted the police patrol who could ride with planters and now and then exercise unlimited force upon recalcitrant or runaway slaves; and then, too, there was always a chance that they themselves might also become planters by saving money, by investment, by the power of good luck; and the only heaven that attracted them was the life of the great Southern planter."
W.E.B. DuBois 1935, Black Reconstruction 1860-1880, Harcourt Brace and Co.

BLACK CONFEDERATES SOLDIERS

This topic, right now, is surely going to ruffle some feathers. Well, if you have read any of my works, or if you know me personally, then you know I don't care. The push is on big time to erase the history of the real relationship between Black people and White people during the civil war. Hollywood, most always, presents this extremist contrast of the old South. Its always the Master /Slave theme or some variation thereof. Even the so called stories about liberated Blacks, they too always revolve around the White slaver and the nigger chattel. Its the same with the Confederacy. There are "academics" as we speak searching for funding trying to write a book denying Black men served in the Confederacy. Black men served as war fighters and not just some 'ole nigger bootblacks. I have come across websites, at so called "universities" hustling for funds, to write books, so that they can spin some more bullshit at the gullible youngsters who attend those "institutions of learning." It is an insult to me personally when I hear this, as my family fought for the Confederacy. Let me clarify, what "Blacks" exactly are academics talking about? Because if you read "Ancestry Lost" then you know "Black" could be anything other than White, and most likely meant "Indian" as well. So here is a current "academic," most likely "teaching" :

"It would be hard to prove that absolutely zero blacks fought in the Confederate army, but I think it must have approached that level. I wonder if "non-white" includes American Indians. I suspect it does and further suspect that American Indians would have been much more prevalent than blacks in Confederate ranks. I haven't kept a count of how many Civil War soldiers' diaries and letters I've read–I guess it has been quite a few–but I've never come across a single instance of a black serving in the Confederate army. Whatever may have been

the number of blacks serving and actually fighting as soldiers in the Confederate army, it must have been a minuscule percentage-completely insignificant for any-one trying to make the argument that blacks saw the conflict as a war of Yankee aggression, felt it was their war too, and joined up to fight for the Confeder-acy. That's just a fairy tale."
Professor and Civil War historian-author Steven Wood-worth History Dept. Texas Christian University

You see, the push is on and "reconstruction" is ongo-ing. It is evidently an extensive focus on this part of history. From the destruction of the Confederate monu-ments to the pundits in media, a lot of people, are pushing foolishness. The part that rubs me wrong is the way is the White historians constantly pump either the Africa theme or the lowly nigger incapable of physical-ly defending "his" nation as well. American originally means "copper colored races," although it is now used by Europeans in America. This is our country as well. How is it possible for some "White academic" with no knowledge of a person's lineage, to tell that person, "You are from Africa, a former slave, a coward boot licker who never fought for his country, except it? That's what happening on every level to people in gen-eral, not just Blacks. People are being given a crock of historical bullshit by these educators and its harm-ing our (ALL) children. I remember being in school and "Roots" coming out. It scared the shit out of me. The teachers were pushing the "out of Africa" bullshit and I went home and told my grandmother and mother, "We're from Africa!." My people laughed at me 'till they had tears running down their faces. Then both of them, in sync, smiles gone, eyes blazing, stated, "We ain't from no G-D damned Africa, we are Opelousas (Attakapas-Opelousa Tribe (Tsipik), dont let nobody tell you dif-ferent!" So here we are now with the "newly recon-structed" Confederacy fairy tale, masquerading as history, that they've been spinning.

Side Note:
Let us not forget, the first man to die for this United States project (American Revolution) in the Boston Massacre was Crispus Attucks : "Even before blacks adopted this "cause," (American Revolution) they were fighting against British tyranny. The most famous of these early black revolutionaries was Crispus Attucks, <u>a runaway half-breed Indian residing in Boston."</u>
A Historic Context for the African American Military Experience U.S. Army Corps of Engineers, USACERL CRRC 98/87 July 1998 p. 27.

So again, the "Indian" is called black, he's a runaway, etc. Run away from where? His tribe? He was not a slave, so run away is a curious description. He was an "American" fighting and dying for "his" land, and against perceived British oppression.

Now back to the issue of Black war fighters in the Confederacy: "To "furnish us with the means of preventing temporary disaster, and carrying on a protracted struggle," he continued, the Army must "immediately commence training a large reserve of the most courageous of our slaves" (MacGregor and Nalty 1977, 2:202 203). President Davis felt that circumstance did not warrant such a radical step and lambasted Cleburne's recommendations as "productive only of discouragement, distraction, and dissension and are to be deeply deprecated" (MacGregor and Nalty 1977, 2:206) In spite of Davis' order to suppress Cleburne's proposal, news of the plan leaked throughout the Confederacy and aroused a lively discussion. Citizens throughout the South were holding meetings, urging the use of blacks as soldiers (Hay 1919: 61-62).

One Georgia slaveholder wrote Davis late in the war

that "many of our wealthy farmers are willing, yea anxious to put their negroes into the war...The crys (sic)
from the suffering widows and orphans demand it, humanity, in behalf of our bleeding country, calls loudly
for help, and there is no other help" (Berlin et al.
1982:286). A fellow planter added that "He who values
his property[slaves] higher than his life and independence is a poor, sordid wretch; a gold worshiper; a
slave in spirit" (MacGregor and Nalty 1977, 2: 211).
Political leaders also seriously contemplated the use
of slaves as a cure for the Army's problems.

In October 1864, five southern governors met in Augusta
to discuss the numerous problems facing the Confederacy. One of the resolutions they passed was support of
Cleburne's proposal to arm the slaves (Quarles 1953:
278-279; Wiley 1938:151). And some of Confederate Con-
gressmen and even some of Davis's cabinet members also
pushed for the plan. The first move toward implementing
this scheme was initiated the following January when
the Virginia legislature authorized the arming of
slaves without promise of emancipation.(Eaton 1954:264)
That same month General Robert E. Lee, commander of the
Confederate Army, "broke the back" (Wiley 1938:158) of
any opposition to the arming of slaves when he wrote
Congress declaring: "I think... we must decide whether
slavery shall be extinguished by our enemies and the
slaves be used against us, or use them ourselves at the
risk of the effect which may be produced upon our social institutions. My own opinion is that we should em-
ploy without delay. I believe that with proper regulations they can be made efficient soldiers (MacGregor
and Nalty 1977, 2:212). USACERL CRRC TR-98/87 53 As the
leading military commander in the Confederate Army (and
a well respected member of Southern society), Lee's
suggestion carried great weight with fellow southerners
(Hay 1919:67). Giving in to such overwhelming military
and public opinion and realizing the desperateness of

their situation, the Confederate Congress passed an act on 13 March allowing the enlistment of slaves into the Army. Each state was to enroll 300,000 slaves (Wesley 1919:251). However, the bill lacked one important element: emancipation for volunteers. Congress left that decision to individual states. (Preisser 1975:103; Wesley 1919:251; Hay 1919:67). The call recruitment quickly went out, but it was far too late. Only one unit of Virginians appears to have engaged in combat in late March, but the war was soon over (Preisser 1975:113 A Historic Context for the African American Military Experience."
U.S. Army Corps of Engineers, USACERL CRRC 98/87 July 1998 p.

"As in all things, 19th-century New Orleans was a world apart from much of the rest of the South. When the Civil War began, it had a large population of so-called free men of color, citizens descended from French and Spanish men, on the one side, and slave women on the other. Colonial-era slave codes granted them complete equality; the "hommes de couleur libre" could own land, businesses and even slaves; they could be educated and serve in the military. They created a niche for themselves in the Crescent City's multicultural society and became important to Louisiana's defense, maintaining their own militia units that served in various Indian wars and against the British during the Revolutionary War. After the United States acquired Louisiana in 1803, the status of the free men of color changed significantly.

Louisiana's Constitution of 1812 specifically restricted the right to vote to white men who owned property. The free men of color could still own property and serve in the militia, but they were left out of politics, and their status began to decline. Nonetheless, they once again volunteered to defend their homes during the War of 1812 and bravely fought for Andrew Jackson at the Battle of New Orleans. (Including my family with the Attakapas Dragoons) A week after civil war erupted in April 1861, some of New Orleans' free men of color offered to form military companies to protect the state against the Union. In an announcement published in the Daily Picayune, the men declared that they were prepared to defend their homes "against any enemy who may come and disturb its tranquility." The Daily Crescent newspaper declared: "Our free colored men … are certainly as much attached to the land of their birth as their white brethren here in Louisiana. … [They] will fight with the Black Republican with as much determination and gallantry as any body of white men in the service of the Confederate States." (Again, my family with the 15th, 16th Louisiana Regiment and the Consolidated Cresecent)

Soon afterward, hundreds of free men of color gathered in the street to show their support for the Confederacy. A regiment known as the Native Guards was soon formed and mustered into the state militia, but the Confederate government refused to accept them into the national army. All of the regiment's line officers were of African descent, although Gov. Thomas O. Moore appointed a white officer to command it. Popular history clams that many of the Native Guards were wealthy slave owners who were members of New Orleans' upper class, but that is not true. While a few might have been well-to-do and owned slaves, and some certainly were related to prominent citizens, the 1860 census shows that a vast majority were clerks, artisans and skilled laborers — lower middle class at the time. The black militia disbanded when Union forces occupied New Orleans in the spring of 1862. After the Battle of Baton Rouge in August, Gen. Benjamin F. Butler, the Union's military governor of Louisiana, requested reinforcements to defend New Orleans, but none were forthcoming. In desperation, Butler informed Secretary of War Edwin M. Stanton that he planned to raise a regiment of free blacks. On Sept. 27, 1862, Butler mustered the First Regiment of Louisiana Native Guards into Union service, making it the first sanctioned regiment of African-American troops in the United States Army. It has generally been assumed that the African-Americans who joined Butler's Native Guards were the same ones who had served earlier in the state militia regiment by the same name. Butler, in fact, claimed that was the case. As a result, historians have questioned the sincerity of the black militiamen who volunteered for Confederate service in 1861. Their supposed change in loyalty seems to indicate that their offer to fight for the South was made only to protect their economic and social status within the community; to not volunteer would make white neighbors suspicious and possibly lead to retaliation. Some Native Guards said as much to Butler and others. Military service records, however, call this assumption into question. Despite Butler's claim to the contrary, a vast majority of his Native Guards were not free men of color but slaves who had made their way into Union lines. James G. Hollandsworth Jr., a professor at the University of Southern Mississippi who wrote the definitive study of the Native Guards, found that only 108 of the 1,035 members of the Louisiana militia regiment, or about 10 percent, went on to serve in the Union's Native Guards. This would seem to indicate that a large number of the black militiamen were indeed sincere in their desire to fight for the South and defend their homes against invasion."

The Free Men of Color Go to War By Terry L. Jones The Free Men of Color Go to War October 19, 2012, New York Times.

"Dr. Lewis Steiner, Chief Inspector of the United States Sanitary Commission, observed General Stonewall Jackson's occupation of Frederick, Maryland, in 1862. He wrote:

Over 3,000 Negroes must be included in this number [of Confederate troops]. These were clad in all kinds of uniforms, not only in cast-off or captured United States uniforms, but in coats with Southern buttons, State buttons, etc. Most of the Negroes had arms, rifles, muskets, sabers, bowie knives, dirks, etc. … and were manifestly an integral portion of the Southern Confederate Army (in Barrow, et al., 2001).

This description of men wearing shell jackets or coats and carrying weapons suggests soldiers. It does not appear indicative of cooks or musicians or body servants. Of course, we cannot know by the description, but it suggests 3,000 armed black Confederate soldiers.

Report of Frederick Douglass:

"There are at the present moment many Colored men in the Confederate Army doing duty not only as cooks, servants and laborers, but real soldiers, having musket on their shoulders, and bullets in their pockets, ready to shoot down any loyal troops and do all that soldiers may do to destroy the Federal government and build up that of the rebels"

(In Williams "On Black Confederates") scvcalifornia.blogspot.com

Recent so called "historians" seem united in their concerted effort to diminish the role of Blacks in the Confederate cause. According to the 1860 census, the population of free blacks residing in the eleven Southern states, which made up the Confederacy, totaled roughly 182,660." Virginia led the largest free black population, followed by North Carolina, Louisiana,

South Carolina, and Tennessee respectively. However, as with the census data for slaves during the war, fluctuations also occurred in the free black population. The previous decade had witnessed a concerted legislative effort throughout the South to curb this perceived threat to slavery, but during the war the movement of refugees, runaways, and further laws all had a part in the displacement of free black southerners. In Virginia, for example, the free black population increased from 54,030 in 1850 to 58,042 in 1860 representing an increase of 7.43 per cent. However, by the second year of the war, this sector of the population had decreased to 48,626 of which only 9,272 or 19.07 per cent were males over the age of twenty-one." In 1861, the Virginia legislature imposed a poll tax on its free black citizeniy as part of its war revenue bill, and of those assessed, 3,328 free blacks were charged with delinquency in payment of the tax, which amounted to $2,702 dollars in lost state revenue. The figures show that the majority of free blacks were able to pay" and in 1862, the state raised the tax from eighty cents to $1.25, which at the end of the fiscal year amounted to $11,500 in extra funds to the public treasury."

"In Louisiana, in late April 1861, the New Orleans Picayune reported, "a meeting often thousand men, representing the flower of the free colored population of New Orleans, and that this meeting resulted in the organization and enrollment of the Louisiana Native Guards." In November under the overall command of Major General Mansfield Lovell, the Guards Regiment, along with their white counterparts marched in review, and it is estimated that therewere more than fourteen hundred blacks in the line of advance."

"In 1862, a regiment of free mulattos was also organized for the defense of New Orleans, and the following year they were taken into the Confederate service as heavy artillery."

"The state's Governor Thomas O.Moore praised the free blacks of the state for their patriotism and requested that their military organization be maintained for the duration of the war. As the war developed into a lengthy struggle, authorities in Louisiana made increasing use of its free black residents. On 11 Februaiy 1864, a law authorized Governor Henry W. Allen to enlist "all Free Men of Color between sixteen and fifty five years into the service of the state."' Free blacks called into service received the same pay and were subject to the same regulations as whites within the same branch of the service. Possible transfer to Confederate service was also authorized, based on consultation and evidence of need."

"On 29 October 1864, Governor Allen issued a General Order which further specified that, "all Free Colored Persons, between eighteen and forty five years of age, and former resident in New Orleans, were required to report at the district enrolling office to be enrolled."

"By the close of the first year of hostilities, at least five of the Confederate states were accepting all able-bodied free blacks into the state militias. One hundred and fifty free black men of Charleston offered their services on 3 January 1861 in throwmg up redoubts wherever necessazy for the protection of the coast. Three months later, the Charleston Mercury reported that several companies of free blacks from Memphis were observed passing through the city. "

"The Memphis Avalanche, on 9 May 1861 contained the following: Artention Volunteers: Resolved by the Committee of Safety that C. Deloach, D. R. Cook; and

William B. Greenlaw be authorized to organize a volunteer company, composed of our patriotic free men of color, of the city of Memphis, for the service of our common defense. All who have not enrolled their names will call at the office of W. B. Greenlaw and Company."

"On 28 June 1861, Tennessee passed a measure recommended by Governor Isham O. Harris "to receive all free male persons of color between fifteen and fifty years of age into the militaiy service of the state. They were to receive eight dollars per month as pay, one ration a day, and a yearly allowance for clothing." The county sheriff held the authority of enforcement, organization, and delivery, and had to report to the Governor the numbers, conditions, and the names of free blacks subject to the law. It was reported that, "several hundred of the free blacks thus raised marched through the streets of Memphis carrying shovels, axes, and blankets. They were evidently quite happy, for they shouted for Jefferson Davis and sang war songs."

Two weeks later, on 17 September 1861, Memphis Avalanche, reported that, "more than a thousand blacks, likewise organized under the act, left the city armed with spades and pick axes, their destination was reported unknown."

"In Georgia, another group of free blacks published an open letter to the district's commanding officer, Bngadier General Alexander Robert Lawton, in the Savannah Evening News. The group had declared that:

The undersigned freemen of color, residing in the city of Savannah and county of Chatham, fully impressed with the feeling of duty we owe to the State of Georgia as inhabitants thereof; which has for so long a period extended to ourselves and families its protection, and has been to us the source of many benefits beg leave, respectfully, in this the hour of danger, to tender to yourself our services, to be employed in the defense of the state, at any place or point, at any time, or any length of time, and in any service for which you may consider us best fitted, andin which we can contribute to the public good."

"In 1862, a Union surgeon who had been caught behind Confederate lines, made the following observation in his diaiy on the movement of the Anny of Northern Virginia as it marched toward Sharpsburg, Matyland, and the accompanying presence of several thousand black Southerners:

At 4 o'clock this morning, the Rebel army began to move from our town, Jackson's force taking the advance. The movement conimued until 8 o'clock P.M., occupying 16 hours. The most liberal calculation could not give them more than 64,000 men. Over 3,000 Negroes must be included in the number... They had arms, rifles, muskets, sabers, bowie knives, dirks, etc. They were supplied, in many instances, with knapsacks, haversacks, canteens, etc., and they were manifestly an integral portion of the Southern Confederacy army. They were seen riding on horses and mules, driving wagons, riding on caissons, in ambulances, with the staff of generals and promiscuously mixed up with all the Rebel horde."

"Not all these men were slaves, as there were also free black body (Body Guards, actually) servants within the ranks who had held either economic or other attachments to the people they served. Many voluntarily became body servants (Body Guards) for wages and whatever other advantages they might negotiate. In addition, self-preservation was for many the paramount objective, and body servants were quite capable of taking full advantage of the situation. (Body guards because the Blacks

were known to be fierce fighters and the rich would often contract a "body servant" to fight alongside and
protect the relative, that's fact.)

Library of Con. -Andrew and Silas Chandler (Free Black)

Take this photo for example. The Confederate Black man
is not a slave. He is more than likely contracted to
fight along side this man. They are both armed, and although the White man is sitting higher, denoting status, the Black Man's rifle is across them both, symbol-
izing protection and unity. Slaves dont possess arms,
and slaves dont dress in Confederate uniforms. These
men were comrads in arms and the Black man was not some
boot lickin' uncle Tom, he, like the White man, was
fighting for his people and his land.

"Prinus Kelly was a slave from North Carolina who moved
to Texas before the War with the family of John W. S.
West They settled in Grimes County, Texas, where they
became successful cotton planters. Kelly grew up with

West's three sons, Robert, Richard, and John, Jr., and when the war started, the sons joined the 8 Texas Cavalry, also now as Terry's Texas Rangers. On the day the regiment boarded a train in Houston to head east, Kelly showed up on his own and went with them. Being black, Kelly was prohibited from officially joining the outfit, however his name does appear on the troops muster sheets as a "colored servant." Yet he donned a gray uniform and carried a gun. Richard was wounded twice in battle, and each time Kelly carried him home to Texas. Each time that Richard returned to the war, Kelly went with him. At Woodsonville, Shiloh, Bardstown, Pertyville, Murfreesboro, Chickamauga, and Knoxville, all four members of the West family fought, black alongside white. After the war Primus Kelly returned to Texas, bought a small farm near his "brothers," and lived there until his death in 1890."

"At the battle of Port Republic, Virginia in June 1862 Edmund Drew, a black barber assigned to the Charlottesville Light Artillery joined the fight after an unnerved Irish substitute named Brown abandoned the battery's advance caisson during a Yankee attack. During the Seven Days' battles near Richmond, a Confederate soldier confessed his frigbt to his superior officer, who disgustedly ordered him to the rear. Westley "a good-looking darkey" received permission to take the coward's place and armed himself with his weapons. Westley provided a good account of himself during the battle, killing a Federal trooper with every shot, which resulted in his being acclaimed as an inspiration to soldiers throughout the regiment."

"One Confederate officer recalled that his servant William "a strong 23 year old and part Indian, was six feet in height, and when with me as bold as a lion, having fought by my side in more than one affair."

"Another officer remembered that at Brandy Station, (Virginia, 9 June 1863) "my Negro servant Edmund, formed the [other] officers' servants, and colored cooks in line immediately in the rear of the regiment and flourishing an old saber over his head,took command of them. As the troops moved into battle their servants went too, but when the artillery shells started landing they scattered in every direction." At the same engagement, two servants from the 12th Virginia Cavalry, who went by the names of Tom and Overton, picked up rifles discarded by Northerners and joined in the charge. They captured the black servant of a Union officer and marched him back to camp, where he was promptly put to work there rather than return him to slavery as stipulated by Confederate policy."

Black Confederate soldier depicted marching in rank
with white Confederate soldiers. This is taken from the
Confederate monument at Arlington National Cemetery.
Designed by Moses Ezekiel, a Jewish Confederate erected
in 1908. Ezekiel depicted the Confederate Army as he
himself witnessed. As such, it is the one of the first
monument, if not the first, honoring a black American
soldier. (Photo by Bob Crowell)

"When Brigadier General George H. Gordon, ordered the

charge at Fort Wagner; on 18 July 1863, he noted that; "there was sharp picket firing from Wagner, in which many men from my command were killed. Strange stories were bruited about of the fatal precision and fire of a Negro marksman, a Rebel." Further collaborative evidence is derived from James H. Goading, a black corporal of the 54th Massachusetts Infantry Regiment who was stationed near Fort Wagner, and one of the few who survived the assault on that Confederate position. Gooding's letters were published "as sent" in his hometown of New Bedford Massachusetts. In this excerpt from a letter dated 30 August 1863, he relates an event of particular interest:

"Last Thursday night [27 August} our pickets were successful in assaulting and carrying the rebel rifle pits, close under Wagner, Among the captured prisoners, were 5 black men; two were fully armed and equipped, as rebel sharpshooters. They had the very best pattern of rifle, "neutral" make, and are represented by the "trash" as unerring shots. The other three were at work in the trenches. One of these sable rebels is represented to be a reb at heart; he is a large owner of chattels himself and does not seem to exhibit any of that humble or cowering mind. There may be many more such men as that in the South; but the idea of Mr. Davis relying on his attached and docile servants to recuperate his wasted annies is all moonshine... The slaves would very likely be glad to get arms, but Mr. Davis probably is certain they would use them on the kind and indulgent upholders of the peculiar institution instead of the marauding Yankees. And if he takes the chattels to fill the army, who is to raise the whittles? Patriotism and dreams of a Great Southern Empire may sustain the spirit of treason, but the rebels are not Joves nor wizards; they must eat. But I hope Mr. Davis may so far forget himself as to call on every able Negro in his so called Confederacy, for it is plain to be seen that they would only be ready to fall into Uncle Sam's ranks at the first opportunity, with the advantage of coining to us armed and equipped, at the expense of the Confederacy, and Neutral Britain."

"There are several accounts of black sharpshooters: some black Southerners evidently had an aptitude for the rifle. During the Peninsula Campaign in 1862, a black sharpshooter appeared firing at troops from Hiram Berdan's U. S. Sharpshooters. The unit's historian later wrote the following, which bears extensive quotation: For a considerable time during the siege the enemy had a Negro rifle shooter in their front who kept up a close fire on our men, and, although the distance was great, yet he caused more or less annoyance by his persistent shooting. On one occasion while at the advanced posts with a detail, the writer with his squad had an opportunity to note the skill of this determined darky with his well aimed rifle. Being stationed at a pit on the edge of a wood fronting the treeless stretch of ground around the opposing works, with sand bags piled up for cover, during the forenoon this rebellious black made his appearance by the side of an officer and under his direction commenced firing at us. For a long time this chance shooting was kept up, the black standing out in plain view and cool drawing bead, but failed to elicit any response, our orders being to lie quiet and not be seen. So the Negro had the shooting all to himself his pop, pop, against the sand bags on the edge of the pit often occurring, while other close shots among the trees showed plainly that he was a good shot at long range. He became pretty well known among the scouts and pickets, and had established quite a reputation for marksmanship, before he came to grief. Emboldened by his having pretty much all this promiscuous shooting unopposed, the pickets rarely firing at him, he began to work at shorter distance, taking advantage of ground and scattering trees. This was what our men

106

wanted, to get him within more reasonable range, not caring to waste ammunition trying to cripple him at the long distance he had at first been showing himself They wanted to make sure of him. In the meantime, our boys would when opportunity offered, without being seen, post a man forward to await in concealment for the adventurous darky. The scheme succeeded and his fate was sealed. A scouting party was sent out, cornered the black sharpshooter in a chimney top a quarter of a mile in front of their lines, and shot him."

"In August of 1861, a Federal officer observed a group he called the "Richmond Howitzer Battery" near Newport News, Virginia that was manned by blacks."

"A correspondent from the New York Times riding with Ulysses S. Grant reported in 1863 on a black artillery crew in Tennessee. "The guns of the rebel battery were manned almost wholly by Negroes," he noted, with "a single white man, or perhaps two, directing operations."

"An Indiana private wrote in a letter to his hometown newspaper about an exchange of fire with a group of black Southerners in the fall of 1861:

A body of seven hundred Negro infantry opened fire on our men, wounding two lieutenants and two privates. The wounded men testify positively that they were shot by Negroes, and that not less than seven hundred were present, aimed with muskets. This is, indeed, a new feature in the war. We have heard of a regiment of Negroes at [First] Manassas and another at Memphis, and still another at New Orleans, but did not believe it till it came so near home and attacked our men. One of the lieutenants was shot in the back of the neck and is not expected to live. "...as excitement over the forthcoming battle at Manassas Junction neared, "all the

colored people"were sent off to the front lines to
fight. Parker arrived at the Junction two days before
the start of the engagement and recalled that, They immediately placed me in one of the batteries. There were
four colored men in our battery, I don't know how many
there were in the others. We opened fire about ten o'-
clock in the morning of Sunday the 2 1; couldn't see
the Yankees at all and only fired at random. Sometimes
they were concealed in the woods. My work was to hand
the balls and swab out the cannon; in this, we took
turns. The officers aimed this gun; we fired grapeshot.
The balls from the Yankee guns fell thick all around.
In one battery a shell burst and killed twenty, the
rest ran. I felt bad all the time, and thought every
minute my time would come; I felt so excited that I
hardly knew what I was about, and felt worse than
dead."

Charles F. Lutz of St. Landxy Parish, Louisiana, was
born in 1842, the son of a white father and mulatto
mother. 1-Ic enlisted in Company F, 8 Louisiana ln-
fantry in 1861, and went to Virginia with the brigade
commanded by General Richard Taylor.' This company
fought at Winchester, Cross Keys, and Port Republic
with Stonewall Jackson in the Valley campaign of
1862, and in the Seven Days, Second Manassas, Sharpsburg, and Fredericksburg battles with Lee and the Army
of Northern Virginia. Lutz was captured at Chancel-
lorsville, Virginia, along with about 100 men from the
regiment. He spent two weeks in prison, was released,
and by June had returned to the Army of Northern Virginia. On the evening of 2 July, he charged up
Cemetery Hill with Hays' Louisiana Brigade. The Confederates overran and captured three Federal lines and
several cannon. They paused to regroup and were soon
attacked by several Federal brigades who held their
fire until within twenty feet of the Louisiana regiment. The volley killed or wounded many Southerners,

including Lutz. He took a bullet in the left arm and was captured for a second time. He was eventually exchanged again, but went home to recuperate from his Gettysburg wound and never returned to Virginia Discharged by the army in May 1865, it was later determined that Lutz was in fact black by the Louisiana Pension Board, but was still able to receive a state pension in 1900."

"William Colen Revels was twenty years old when he volunteered for Confederate service, and was one of the first men of any color in Suny County, North Carolina, to march off to war. He spent the greater part of the war in the 21 North Carolina Infantry, and is listed on the rolls as a "Negro." He was wounded in the leg at Winchester, and caught a bullet in the right thigh at Gettysburg, probably on East Cemetery Hill on 2 July 1863. Although there were at least five black Southerners who served in the regiment, Revels was the only one that could be documented as having served at Gettysburg." These was also a report of several slaves and free blacks who marched there"

"... the 14th Tennessee, and 13th Alabama Infantry Regiments... These men apparently fell into line with General James J. Archer's Brigade and helped open the battle on 1 July. On the 3" day of the battle, they formed the center of the line led by Colonel B. D. Fry. Here a "black Corporal" picked up a Confederate flag near the Emmitsburg Road, climbed over the fences and charged up the ridge, only to be shot just before reaching the stone wall."

"In addition, the New York Herald reported that on 1 July 1863 a group of armed black men were captured, and "among the rebel prisoners who were marched through Gettysburg, there were observed seven negroes in uniform and fully accoutered as soldiers."

"...at Williamsport, Mayland, waiting for the water to recede, Union artillery began shelling their position. As he turned toward the wagons, the officer suddenly was aware that not a single teamster was to be seen. He could not account for until he happened to look toward the river, and there saw hundreds of black heads just showing above the water. "The Negro teamsters with one accord had plunged into the river to escape the shells, and were submerged to the neck!"

"When the Union advance appeared before Williamsport, on 7 July 1863, another Confederate officer witnessed that the black Southerners attached to the train, "probably 500 teamsters in all, were organized into companies, and armed with the weapons of the wounded men found in the train." Slightly wounded officers, quartermasters, and commissaries were pressed into service to lead them. Combined with roughly 2100 regular soldiers they stood off a much larger enemy force headed by cavalry Generals John Buford, and Hugh Judson Kilpatrick. "This came to be known as 'the wagoner's fight' in our army from the fact that so many of them [blacks] were armed' and did such gallant service in repelling the attack made on our right."

"However, on 13 March 1865, after several months of official debate in the Confederate Congress, the government finally began actively recruiting and enlisting black soldiers. From the moment the new act was passed, messages were sent out authorizing state governors and field commanders to begin raising black troops, and soon drilling was taking place in several areas of the unoccupied South. Indeed, on the same day, "two companies [of black Confederates] were seen parading with a battalion."

"Another witness recorded that "the Confederate Veteran, vol. II, no 4, (April 1894), p. 117...streets of

Richmond were filled with 10,000 Negroes who had been gathered at Camp Lee on the outskirts of Richmond. The negroes were armed and placed in trenches near Richmond."

"By 1865, the few slaves and free blacks who were still acting as either support staff or as military laborers, now made the formal transition to a combat role. Thomas Morris Chester, a black newspaper correspondent from Philadelphia, was near Richmond at this time, and had interviewed several blacks soon after the fall of the city. He recorded that the black community was abuzz with a discussion of how they should react to the call to arms. That, "after a cordial exchange of opinions it was decided with great unanimity, and finally ratified by all the auxiliary associations everywhere, that black men should promptly respond to the call of the rebel chiefs, whenever it should be made, for them to take up arms."

"Richmond's vast hospitals were a prime source of recruits. One writer observed, "The Battalion from Camps Winder and Jackson, under the command of Dr. Chambliss, paraded on the square each Wednesday evening." The doctor made particular note that, "this was the first company of Negro Troops raised in Virginia" "It was organized about a month since, by Dr. Chainbliss, from the employees of the hospitals and served on the lines during the recent Sheridan raid." Major Thomas P. Turner subsequently raised another company of black Southerners, which was drilled daily in Richmond's square by Lieutenant Virginius Bossieux."

"On 27 March, the Richmond Examiner reported that the company numbered 35 men, with new members coming in every day. The men were busily recruiting their friends, and it seemed that "the knowledge of the military art they already exhibit was something remarkable. They moved with evident pride and satisfaction to themselves. Their quarters in the rendezvous are neat, clean, warm, and comfortable, and their rations were cooked at Libby Prison."

"By late March 1865, a few black Southerners finally saw combat in authorized Confederate units. Some units were seen at various points during the retreat to Appomattox, and one even stood up to forward units under the command of Union General Philip Sheridan. One white lieutenant of a black company noted, "my men acted with the utmost promptness and good will. Allow me to state, Sir, that they behaved in an extraordinary suitable manner."'

"A Virginia private watched as one black unit, guarding a Confederate wagon train during the retreat was threatened by Federal cavalry, and witnessed that their initial defense made by the black soldiers proved successful. The Union soldiers retreated, but reformed on a nearby hillside, then proceeded to charge down on the wagon train, move in, and capture the black Confederates."

"An army courier further reported that on 4 April 1865 he saw black Southerners working on breastworks. "All wore good gray uniforms and I was informed that they belonged to the only company of colored troops in the Confederate service, having been enlisted by Major Turner in Richmond. Their muskets were stacked, and it was evident that they regarded their present employment in no very favorable light."

"Despite these attempts at recruiting and utilizing slaves and free blacks as soldiers the Confederate authorities were too late to change the course of the war, or to produce a desired victory over a massive Federal presence."

Wearing The Gray Suit: Black Enlistment and the Confederate Military Frank Edward Deserino, University of London Department of History, University College London July, 2001

Here are some more noted examples:

1. The "Richmond Howitzers" were partially manned by black militiamen. They saw action at 1st Manassas (or 1st Battle of Bull Run) where they operated battery no. 2. In addition two black "regiments", one free and one slave, participated in the battle on behalf of the South. "Many colored people were killed in the action", recorded John Parker, a former slave.

2. At least one Black Confederate was a non-commissioned officer. James Washington, Co. D 35th Texas Cavalry, Confederate States Army, became it's 3rd Sergeant. Higher ranking black commissioned officers served in militia units, but this was on the State militia level (Louisiana) and not in the regular C.S. Army.

3. Free black musicians, cooks, soldiers and teamsters earned the same pay as white confederate privates. This was not the case in the Union army where blacks did not receive equal pay. At the Confederate Buffalo Forge in Rockbridge County, Virginia, skilled black workers "earned on average three times the wages of white Confederate soldiers and more than most Confederate army officers ($350- $600 a year).

4. Dr. Lewis Steiner, Chief Inspector of the United States Sanitary Commission while observing Gen. "Stonewall" Jackson's occupation of Frederick, Maryland, in 1862: "Over 3,000 Negroes must be included in this number [Confederate troops]. These were clad in

all kinds of uniforms, not only in cast-off or captured United States uniforms, but in coats with Southern buttons, State buttons, etc. These were shabby, but not shabbier or seedier than those worn by white men in the rebel ranks. Most of the Negroes had arms, rifles, muskets, sabers, bowie-knives, dirks, etc.....and were manifestly an integral portion of the Southern Confederate Army."

5. Frederick Douglas reported, "There are at the present moment many Colored men in the Confederate Army doing duty not only as cooks, servants and laborers, but real soldiers, having musket on their shoulders, and bullets in their pockets, ready to shoot down any loyal troops and do all that soldiers may do to destroy the Federal government and build up that of the rebels."

6. Black and white militiamen returned heavy fire on Union troops at the Battle of Griswoldsville (near Macon, GA). Approximately 600 boys and elderly men were killed in this skirmish.

7. In 1864, President Jefferson Davis approved a plan that proposed the emancipation of slaves, in return for the official recognition of the Confederacy by Britain and France. France showed interest but Britain refused.

8. The Jackson Battalion included two companies of black soldiers. They saw combat at Petersburg under Col. Shipp. "My men acted with utmost promptness and goodwill...Allow me to state sir that they behaved in an extraordinary acceptable manner."

9. Recently the National Park Service, with a recent discovery, recognized that blacks were asked to help defend the city of Petersburg, Virginia and were offered their freedom if they did so. Regardless of their

official classification, black Americans performed support functions that in today's army many would be classified as official military service. The successes of white Confederate troops in battle, could only have been achieved with the support these loyal black Southerners.

10. Confederate General John B. Gordon (Army of Northern Virginia) reported that all of his troops were in favor of Colored troops and that it's adoption would have "greatly encouraged the army". Gen. Lee was anxious to receive regiments of black soldiers. The Richmond Sentinel reported on 24 Mar 1864, "None...will deny that our servants are more worthy of respect than the motley hordes which come against us." "Bad faith [to black Confederates] must be avoided as an indelible dishonor."

11. In March 1865, Judah P. Benjamin, Confederate Secretary Of State, promised freedom for blacks who served from the State of Virginia. Authority for this was finally received from the State of Virginia and on April 1st 1865, $100 bounties were offered to black soldiers. Benjamin exclaimed, "Let us say to every Negro who wants to go into the ranks, go and fight, and you are free...Fight for your masters and you shall have your freedom." Confederate Officers were ordered to treat them humanely and protect them from "injustice and oppression".

12. A quota was set for 300,000 black soldiers for the Confederate States Colored Troops. 83% of Richmond's male slave population volunteered for duty. A special ball was held in Richmond to raise money for uniforms for these men. Before Richmond fell, black Confederates in gray uniforms drilled in the streets. Due to the war ending, it is believed only companies or squads of these troops ever saw any action. Many more black sol-

diers fought for the North, but that difference was simply a difference because the North instituted this progressive policy more sooner than the more conservative South. Black soldiers from both sides received discrimination from whites who opposed the concept.

13. Union General U.S. Grant in Feb 1865, ordered the capture of "all the Negro men… before the enemy can put them in their ranks." Frederick Douglas warned Lincoln that unless slaves were guaranteed freedom (those in Union controlled areas were still slaves) and land bounties, "they would take up arms for the rebels".

14. On April 4, 1865 (Amelia County, VA), a Confederate supply train was exclusively manned and guarded by black Infantry. When attacked by Federal Cavalry, they stood their ground and fought off the charge, but on the second charge they were overwhelmed. These soldiers are believed to be from "Major Turner's" Confederate command.

15. A Black Confederate, George, when captured by Federals was bribed to desert to the other side. He defiantly spoke, "Sir, you want me to desert, and I ain't no deserter. Down South, deserters disgrace their families and I am never going to do that."

16. Former slave, Horace King, accumulated great wealth as a contractor to the Confederate Navy. He was also an expert engineer and became known as the "Bridge builder of the Confederacy." One of his bridges was burned in a Yankee raid. His home was pillaged by Union troops, as his wife pleaded for mercy.

17. One black C. S. Navy seaman was among the last Confederates to surrender, aboard the CSS Shenandoah, six months after the war ended. At least two blacks served as Navy pilots with the rank of Warrant Officer. One,

116

William Bugg, piloted the CSS Sampson, and another, Moses Dallas, was considered the best inland pilot of the C.S. Navy. Dallas piloted the Savannah River squadron and was paid $100 a month until the time he was killed by the enemy during the capture of USS Water Witch.

18. Nearly 180,000 Black Southerners, from Virginia alone, provided logistical support for the Confederate military. Many were highly skilled workers. These included a wide range of jobs: nurses, military engineers, teamsters, ordnance department workers, brakemen, firemen, harness makers, blacksmiths, wagonmakers, boatmen, mechanics, wheelwrights, ect. In the 1920'S Confederate pensions were finally allowed to some of those workers that were still living. Many thousands more served in other Confederate States.

19. During the early 1900's, many members of the United Confederate Veterans (UCV) advocated awarding former slaves rural acreage and a home. There was hope that justice could be given those slaves that were once promised "forty acres and a mule" but never received any. In the 1913 Confederate Veteran magazine published by the UCV, it was printed that this plan "If not Democratic, it is [the] Confederate" thing to do. There was much gratitude toward former slaves, which "thousands were loyal, to the last degree", now living with total poverty of the big cities. Unfortunately, their proposal fell on deaf ears on Capitol Hill.

20. During the 5oth Anniversary of the Battle of Gettysburg in 1913, arrangements were made for a joint reunion of Union and Confederate veterans. The commission in charge of the event made sure they had enough accommodations for the black Union veterans, but were completely surprised when unexpected black Confederates arrived. The white Confederates immediately welcomed

their old comrades, gave them one of their tents, and "saw to their every need". Nearly every Confederate reunion including those blacks that served with them, wearing the gray.

21. The first military monument in the US Capitol that honors an African-American soldier is the Confederate monument at Arlington National cemetery. The monument was designed 1914 by Moses Ezekiel, a Jewish Confederate. Who wanted to correctly portray the "racial make-up" in the Confederate Army. A black Confederate soldier is depicted marching in step with white Confederate soldiers. Also shown is one "white soldier giving his child to a black woman for protection".- source: Edward Smith, African American professor at the American University, Washington DC.

22. Black Confederate heritage is beginning to receive the attention it deserves.For instance, Terri Williams, a black journalist for the Suffolk "Virginia Pilot" newspaper, writes: "I've had to re-examine my feelings toward the [Confederate] flag…It started when I read a newspaper article about an elderly black man whose ancestor worked with the Confederate forces. The man spoke with pride about his family member's contribution to the cause, was photographed with the [Confederate] flag draped over his lap…that's why I now have no definite stand on just what the flag symbolizes, because it no longer is their history, or my history, but our history.

Tampa, Florida   Confederate Reunion, early 1900s.

Civil War Drawing of Black Confederate Soldiers

Free Black Confederate Soldier Pvt. Marlboro

United Confederates Reunion 1918 Dallas, Texas

Louis Napoleon Nelson poses with grandson Nelson W. Winbush at the Memphis train station in 1932 before leaving to attend a Confederate reunion celebration.

Louis Napoleon Nelson was born in 1846 in Ripley, Lauderdale County, TN. He died in 1934 at the age of 88. Louis served in an integrated unit for the Confederacy; the 7th Tennessee Cavalry Company M. Louis is a well-known Ripley native due to the efforts of his grandson. According to his grandson, Nelson Winbush, Louis Napoleon Nelson went to war with the sons of his owner, James Oldham, *as their bodyguard*. At first Louis served as a cook and look out, but he later saw action under

the command of General Nathan Bedford Forrest. Louis
also went on to serve as a Chaplain. He could not read
or write, yet he had managed to memorize the King James
Bible. He went on to serve as Chaplain for the next 4
campaigns, leading services with the soldiers before
they went to the battlefield. He fought in battles at
Shiloh, Lookout Mountain, Brice's Crossroads, and
Vicksburg. After the war Louis lived as a freeman on
the James Oldham plantation for several years. He built
a yellow, two story house, with a wraparound porch in
Ripley. Throughout the years Louis went to 39 Confederate reunions proudly wearing his Civil War uniform.
When Louis Napoleon Nelson passed away a Confederate
flag draped his coffin. According to a story in the
Memphis Commercial Appeal newspaper in 1933 Louis described himself as the only colored Democrat in Lauderdale County, TN. His funeral the following year,
which included a military procession, was described as
"the largest colored folks funeral we had ever seen in
our time." Today his story lives on through his grandson Nelson Winbush, who proudly proclaims his grandfather's legacy. SOURCE: Richens, Mark. "'Takeaway' Segment on Black Confederate Soldiers." *Links to Memphis*.
Scripps Interactive Newspapers Group, 12 Apr. 2011.
Web. 01 Oct. 2011.

Holt Collier Company 1, 9th Texas Calvary, post war.
Collier was born a slave. He was in the keep of General
Thomas Hinds, veteran of the Battle of New Orleans.
When the War Between The States began, Collier's master
and his seventeen year-old son, Collier's childhood
companion, left for the war to thwart the Northern ag-
gressors. His master had forbade him to fight in the
ranks of the Confederate service as he was too young.
Collier disobeyed and stowed away on a riverboat, join-

ing another Southern Patriot and his son in Memphis. Collier thereafter joined the 9th Texas Cavalry, serving in Company I throughout the war. At the Battle of Pittsburg Landing{Shiloh} he witnessed the death of Confederate General Albert Sidney Johnston. Collier's biographer says that although there was a prohibition against blacks serving in uniform, Confederates made an exception for Collier because of his demonstrable skills. Weeks later he signed up with Company I of the 9th Cavalry Regiment (United States), fighting in Mississippi, Alabama and Tennessee.

During Reconstruction, Collier was accused and acquitted by a military tribunal in Vicksburg of the alleged murder of a white man, Captain James King. Collier left the state on the advice of William A. Percy of Greenville, going to Texas to work as a cowboy on the ranch of his former commander, Sullivan Ross, future Governor of Texas. Upon the murder of his former master, Collier returned to Greenville for his funeral and remained in Greenville for the rest of his life. He became a noted bear hunter, killing over 3,000 bears during his lifetime. So famous among big-game hunters was he that Major George M. Helm asked him to serve as President Theodore Roosevelt's tracker during the President's famous Mississippi bear hunt of 1902. On that hunt, Collier and his tracking dogs cornered a large bear. Collier had bugled Roosevelt and the rest of his party to join in. Before Roosevelt arrived, the bear killed one of Collier's tracking dogs. Collier ordinarily would have shot the bear immediately, but, wanting to keep the bear alive until the President arrived, he instead whacked the bear over the head with his rifle — bending its barrel. He finally lassoed the bear and tied it to a tree. When the President at last arrived, he famously refused to shoot the helpless bear, which another of his party eventually killed with a knife. The Washington Post and other newspapers publicized Roosevelt's compassion for the animal. Some reports maintained, erroneously, that the bear had been a cub. The story eventually gave rise to the "Teddy Bear" phenomenon. Collier served again as Roosevelt's tracker during a Louisiana bear hunt of 1907. Holt Collier National Wildlife Refuge in Mississippi is named in his honor. He died in 1936 and is buried in Greenville, Mississippi.

" Attack on Our Soldiers by Armed Negroes ! A member of the Indiana Twentieth Regiment, now encamped near Fortress Monroe, writes to the Indianapolis Journal on the 23rd. Yesterday morning General Mansfield with Drake de Kay, Aide-DE-Camp in command of seven companies of the 20th New York, German Riffles, left Newport News on a reconnaissance. Just after passing New Market Bridge, seven miles from camp, they detached one company as an advance, and soon after their advance was attacked by 600 of the enemy's cavalry. The company formed to receive cavalry, but the CAVALRY ADVANCING deployed to the right and left when within musket range and unmasked a body of seven hundred NEGRO INFANTRY, all armed with muskets, who opened fire on our men, wounding two lieutenants and two privates, and rushing forward surrounded the company of Germans who cut their way through killing six of the Negroes and wounding several more. The main body, hearing the firing, advanced at a double-quick in time to recover their wounded, and drive the enemy back, but did not succeed in taking any prisoners. The wounded men TESTIFY POSITIVELY that they were shot by Negroes, and that not less than seven hundred were present, armed with muskets. This is, indeed, a new feature in the war. We have heard of a regiment of Negroes at Manassas, and another at Memphis, and still another at New Orleans but did not believe it till it came so near home, and attacked our men. THERE IS NO MISTAKE ABOUT IT. The 20th German were actually attacked and fired on and wounded by Negroes. It is time that this thing was understood, and if they fight us with Negroes, why should not we fight them with Negroes too? We have disbelieved these reports too long, and now let us fight the devil with fire. The feeling is intense among the men. They want to know if they came here to fight Negroes, and if they did, they would like to know it. The wounded men swear they will kill any Negro they see, so excited are they at the dastardly act. It remains to be seen how long the Government will now hesitate, when they learn these facts. One of the Lieutenants was shot in the back part of the neck, and is not expected to live."

That, I believe supports my position that Blacks did in fact fight for the Confederacy, and I say also in every armed conflict on this continent. A few more Civil War Era quotes:

"If they {the North} prevail, the whole character of the Government will be changed, and instead of a federal republic, the common agent of sovereign and independent States, we shall have a central despotism, with the notion of States forever abolished, deriving its powers from the will, and shaping its policy according to the wishes, of a numerical majority of the people; we shall have, in other words, a supreme, irresponsible democracy. The Government does not now recognize itself as an ordinance of God, and when all the checks and balances of the Constitution are gone, we may easily figure to ourselves the career and the destiny of this godless monster of democratic absolutism. The progress of regulated liberty on this continent will be arrested, anarchy will soon succeed, and the end will be a military despotism, which preserves order by the sacrifice of the last vestige of liberty. They are now fighting the battle of despotism. They have put their

Constitution under their feet; they have annulled its most sacred provisions; The future fortunes of our children, and of this continent, would then be determined by a tyranny which has no parallel in history."
Dr. James Henly Thornwell of South Carolina, in Our Danger and our Duty, 1862

"Every man should endeavor to understand the meaning of subjugation before it is too late... It means the history of this heroic struggle will be written by the enemy; that our youth will be trained by Northern school teachers; will learn from Northern school books their version of the war; will be impressed by the influences of history and education to regard our gallant dead as traitors, and our maimed veterans as fit objects for derision... It is said slavery is all we are fighting for, and if we give it up we give up all. Even if this were true, which we deny, slavery is not all our enemies are fighting for. It is merely the pretense to establish sectional superiority and a more centralized form of government, and to deprive us of our rights and liberties."
Maj. General Patrick R. Cleburne, C.S.A. January 1864.

"When the South raised its sword against the Union's Flag, it was in defense of the Union's Constitution."
Confederate General John B. Gordon

"So the case stands, and under all the passion of the parties and the cries of battle lie the two chief moving causes of the struggle. Union means so many millions a year lost to the South; secession means the loss of the same millions to the North. The love of money is the root of this as of many many other evils ... the quarrel between North and South is, as it stands, solely a fiscal quarrel."
Charles Dickens, as editor of All the Year Round, a British periodical in 1862.

In conclusion of this topic, the civil war war a nasty affair, with close to a million killed and maimed. It is an insult to the memory of all those men and women who died, in order for everyone to have the life that they do now, for so called academics to collude to remove the memory of an entire segment of that conflict. This type of foolishness is what presents itself as "education." Again, the push is on to change the reality of Black life into some coon fairy tale where the nigger is always taking a loss. This has decimated the esteem of Black children and White children as well.

To add a bit more fuel to this fire I would like to present a list of "just my family" who proudly served their Land:

Guillory, A.	Cpl. 59	4 1 6	Guillory, Adolph
Guillory, A.	Cpl. 55	1 2 0 7	Gillory, Aurelian
Guillory, A. V.	Cpl. 59	4 2 6 1 7	Guillory, Marguerite E. O.
Guillory, Achille V.	Cpl. 59	4 2 6 1 7	Guillory, Marguerite E. O.
Guillory, Adolph	Cpl. 59	4 1 6	Guillory, Adolph
Guillory, Alcide	Cpl. 59	4 1 0 1 2	Guillory, Delphine M.
Guillory, Alezier (Jeansonne)	Cpl. 59	4 2 1 1	Guillory, Alezier (Jeansonne)
Guillory, Alida (Soileau)	Cpl. 59	4 3 2	Guillory, Alide (Soileau)
Guillory, Angelina	Cpl. 59	4 4 6	Guillory, Angelina
Guillory, Aris-	Cpl. 59	4 5 1	Guillory, Aris-

Name	Ref				Name
tide	59			3	tide
Guillory, August	Cpl. 59	4	6	4	Guillory, August
Guillory, Augustave	Cpl. 59	4	33	4	Guillory, Ophelia
Guillory, Auguste	Cpl. 59	4	33	4	Guillory, Ophelia
Guillory, Aurelian	Cpl. 55	1	20	7	Gillory, Aurelian
Guillory, Azeline	Cpl. 59	4	7	4	Guillory, Azeline
Guillory, Bruno	Cpl. 59	4	8	9	Guillory, Bruno
Guillory, Celima (Soileau)	Cpl. 59	4	9	11	Guillory, Celina
Guillory, Celina (Soileau)	Cpl. 59	4	9	11	Guillory, Celina
Guillory, D. Cyprian	Cpl. 59	4	23	26	Guillory, Louise G.
Guillory, D. Cyprien	Cpl. 59	4	23	26	Guillory, Louise G.
Guillory, Celina (Soileau)	Cpl. 59	4	9	11	Guillory, Celina
Guillory, D. Cyprian	Cpl. 59	4	23	26	Guillory, Louise G.
Guillory, D. Cyprien	Cpl. 59	4	23	26	Guillory, Louise G.
Guillory, Delphine (Moreau)	Cpl. 59	4	10	12	Guillory, Delphine M.
Guillory, Domitile (Ortego)	Cpl. 59	4	11	4	Guillory, Domitile (Ortego)
Guillory, Donatien	Cpl. 60	1	6	8	Guillory, Vitaline

132

C.	59	8	C.
Guillory, J. P.	Cp1.59	4 1 9 6	Guillory, J. P.
Guillory, Jean Baptiste	Cp1.59	4 2 1 1	Guillory, Alezier (Jeansonne)
Guillory, Jean Baptiste D.	Cp1.59	4 3 1 2 9	Guillory, Odile (Ortego)
Guillory, Jean Bte. D.	Cp1.59	4 3 1 2 9	Guillory, Odile (Ortego)
Guillory, Jean Pierre	Cp1.59	4 1 9 6	Guillory, J
Guillory, Joachim G.	Cp1.59	4 9 1 1	Guillory, Celina
Guillory, Joseph	Cp1.59	4 2 0 2	Guillory, Josephine (Brulte')
Guillory, Joseph	Cp1.59	4 2 5 2	Guillory, Marguerite
Guillory, Joseph	Cp1.59	4 3 5 9	Guillory, Ortelia
Guillory, Josephine (Brulte')	Cp1.59	4 2 0 2	Guillory, Josephine (Brulte')
Guillory, Julien	Cp1.59	4 2 1 9	Guillory, Julien J.
Guillory, Julien D.	Cp1.59	4 2 2 1 3	Guillory, Julien D.
Guillory, Julien J.	Cp1.59	4 2 1 9	Guillory, Julien J.
Guillory, Julien L.	Cp1.130	0 0 9	Guillory, Julien L.
Guillory, Julien L.	Cp1.130	0 0 1 4	Soileau, Eulalie (Lahaye) Guillory
Guillory, L. A.	Cp1.59	4 1 0 1 2	Guillory, Delphine M.

Name	Ref			Related Name
Guillory, L. A.	Cp1.59	4	14 17	Guillory, Elvira E.
Guillory, L. Alcide	Cp1.59	4	14 17	Guillory, Elvira E.
Guillory, Louis Acibiode	Cp1.59	4	14 17	Guillory, Elvira E.
Guillory, Louis Alcide	Cp1.59	4	10 12	Guillory, Delphine M.
Guillory, Louis Alcide	Cp1.59	4	14 17	Guillory, Elvira E.
Guillory, Louise (Gaspard)	Cp1.59	4	23 26	Guillory, Louise G.
Guillory, M'tor	Cp1.59	4	27 15	Guillory, Mentor J.
Guillory, Marceline Soileau	Cp1.59	4	24 5	Guillory, Marceline Soileau
Guillory, Marguerite (Bordelon)	Cp1.59	4	25 2	Guillory, Marguerite
Guillory, Neuville	Cp1.59	4	28 4	Guillory, Neuville
Guillory, Neville	Cp1.59	4	3 2	Guillory, Alide (Soileau)
Guillory, O.	Cp1.59	4	11 4	Guillory, Domitile (Ortego)
Guillory, O. P.	Cp1.59	4	7 4	Guillory, Azeline
Guillory, Octave	Cp1.59	4	30 5	Guillory, Octave
Guillory, Octave	Cp1.60	1	3 5	Guillory, Pierre Eline

Name	Source	No.	Cross-reference
Guillory, Octavo	Cp1. 59	43015	Guillory, Octave
Guillory, Odile (Ortego)	Cp1. 59	43129	Guillory, Odile (Ortego)
Guillory, Olen	Cp1. 59	4114	Guillory, Domitile (Ortego)
Guillory, Oliver P.	Cp1. 59	4296	Guillory, O. P.
Guillory, Olivier P.	Cp1. 59	474	Guillory, Azeline
Guillory, Omarine	Cp1. 59	43210	Guillory, Omarine
Guillory, Onerine	Cp1. 59	43210	Guillory, Omarine
Guillory, Ophelia (Soileau)	Cp1. 59	4334	Guillory, Ophelia
Guillory, Ophelia Bihm (Thibodeaux)	Cp1. 59	4347	Guillory, Ophelia (Thibodeaux)
Guillory, Ortelia (Guillory)	Cp1. 59	4359	Guillory, Ortelia
Guillory, Paul	Cp1. 59	4124	
Guillory, Paul	Cp1. 60	116	
Guillory, Paul, Mrs.	Cp1. 60	116	Guillory, Paul, Mrs.
Guillory, Paulasten	Cp1. 60	116	Guillory, Paul, Mrs.
Guillory, Pauline (Fontenot)	Cp1. 60	124	Guillory, Pauline
Guillory, Pierre	Cp1. 59	43129	Guillory, Odile (Ortego)
Guillory, Pierre Aline (Arnaud)	Cp1. 60	135	Guillory, Pierre Eline

Guillory, Pierre Eline (Arnaud)	Cpl. 60	1 3 5	Guillory, Pierre Eline
Guillory, Pierre Jean Pierre	Cpl. 60	1 4 5	Guillory, Pierre Jean P.
Guillory, Treville D.	Cpl. 59	4 4 6	Guillory, Angelina
Guillory, Treville D.	Cpl. 60	1 5 9	Guillory, Treville D.
Guillory, Valcour V.	Cpl. 59	4 2 1 6 7	Guillory, Marguerite E. O.
Guillory, Vitaline (Roy)	Cpl. 60	1 6 8	Guillory, Vitaline
Guillory, Zelien D.	Cp		

That list is just of Guillory's in Louisiana. It would be silly to assume that no other Black folks fought for the Confederacy.

Side Note: My family did not play politics one way or the other, we were Confederates by default, as we were fighting for our homes and land, which happened to fall under the Confederate territory. The story would have been reversed had they lived North. The tradition within the Guillory clan, both Black and White, of being fighters in Louisiana goes back before the "American Revolution" and in the Revolution with Galvez at the Battle of Baton Rouge:

Galvez' Army. Later that same year, 1779, Spain entered the war as an ally of France against the British. Since 1762, New Orleans and all of Louisiana west of the Mississippi belonged to Spain and it was from here that they attacked the British. Among the Spanish forces were companies of free black militiamen, heirs to the legacy of the 1736 French war with the Chickasaw and Natchez Indians. Under the command of Bernardo de

Galvez, a small army of 750 men (about 100 of whom were black), succeeded in capturing Fort Charlotte at Mobile and Fort George in Pensacola and eventually driving the British from Louisiana and West Florida (McConnell 1968:15-22). By cutting off British access to the west and engaging troops that might have otherwise been employed elsewhere, Galvez' army, and the black troops in it, made a significant contribution to American victory (Nalty 1986:17). From the time of the earliest permanent settlements in North America to the Civil War, African Americans participated in every major military conflict. Denied military service during peacetime, they were actively recruited at the commencement of hostilities. Blacks responded to these calls-to-arms in large numbers. Many saw military service as a way to improve their own condition. Others enlisted in hope that their participation would prove to whites that African Americans deserved equal rights. Unfortunately for these men, their honorable and distinctive military service failed to elevate their status or that of other blacks. Instead, their experiences are replete with disappointment and irony. During the Revolution, for example, many African Americans fought for an independence denied to them. Surprisingly, however, the vast majority of black soldiers were not ostracized from whites; instead, they were placed in integrated units, often receiving equal pay. (This integration policy ended with the Civil War, and did not resurface for almost another 100 years.) Without the service of blacks, the American military successes might not have been possible; still, their contributions were quickly forgotten after each war when they were once again excluded from military service—until the next conflict." Id, USACERL CRRC TR-98/87 pp. 40.

WHY DOES ALL THIS HISTORY MATTER?

It matters because over generations, people of all colors, have been fed a fairy tale about the history of this nation. At some point in the past, as is now, there may have been a national interest in spinning a crock of bullshit at the people, I get it. But over generations, the ongoing and continuous bullshit has driven the populace onto the brink of utter madness. The populace has become a functioning mental patient and the world is the mental ward. "Why do lies or omitted facts matter?" When lies are told it is normally to gain advantage, and when material facts are expunged, then one would deduce the same. Has not an advantage been achieved? Once an advantage is achieved, the ongoing and continuous, unnecessary historical alterations only degrades the foundation of the gained advantage by pro-offering fairy tales for dissection. It matters because over the generations children have been indoctrinated into a fairy tale mind state. These children grow up, become adults and they function 100% within that fairy tale reality. Children are not born with a concept of race, it is taught to them via observation. Children observe the behaviors of others, the speech, inter alia, the body language, the energy, the folk tales (oral traditions), the harmonics of the voice, the interactions between people and most importantly history.

The subliminal messages in fabricated history being taught had reduced and debased the current populace down to the level of feudal Moorish and European tribes of yesterday. Pretend for one second that you hatched out of an egg right now, fully grown, knowing absolutely nothing about the world. You did not know any history, fake or not, you did not know anything... Right now, look at all the adults you see, everywhere. A lot of people are nuts, and you have to ask yourself,

"What the hell happened to them in childhood??" Who raised these people? Where did they get educated? Its been this way for generations and it gets worse each generation. That's because, it's like an actor doing the same old tired show, after awhile its painful to watch. The show, over generations is driving people into mental illness, and to be honest, over the long term , its the only result that can happen....

"California ranks No. 1 among the 50 states for the percentage of its residents 25 and older who have never completed ninth grade and 50th for the percentage who have graduated from high school, according to new data from the Census Bureau.

9.7 percent of California residents 25 and older, the Census Bureau says, never completed ninth grade. Only 82.5 percent graduated from high school. In fact, the 2,510,370 California residents 25 and older who, according to the Census Bureau, never finished ninth grade outnumber the entire populations of 15 other states. In California, children are required to attend school from six years of age until they are 18. "California's compulsory education laws require children between six and eighteen years of age to attend school, with a limited number of exceptions," says the California Legislative Analyst's Office, an agency of the California state government. (The National Center for Education Statistics also indicates that children in California are compelled by law to attend school from 6 to 18 years of age.)"
By Terence P. Jeffrey | December 19, 2018 (CNSNews.com)

That story makes my point. When you couple those "academic" numbers with fairy tales, that people are acting upon, then you have a recipe for disaster. The history of this nation is full of ill, murderous, wretched, shameful behavior and good as well. People need to know

it so they can heal. Mental illness, and every facet
it encompasses, is at an all time high. Where did these
people grow up? How did this many people get broken?
How are these people going to be fixed from now on?

"Central to this understanding is the fact that schools
are not failing. On the contrary, they are spectacular-
ly successful in doing precisely what they are intended
to do, and what they have been intended to do since
their inception."
JOHN TAYLOR GATTO (12-15-35 - 10-25-18)
New York City Teacher of the Year in 1989, 1990, and
1991, and New York State Teacher of the Year in 1991.

"Our form of compulsory schooling is an invention of
the State of Massachusetts around 1850. It was resisted
— sometimes with guns — by an estimated eighty percent
of the Massachusetts population, the last outpost in
Barnstable on Cape Cod not surrendering its children
until the 1880s, when the area was seized by militia
and children marched to school under guard."

"A large fraction of our total economy has grown up
around providing service and counseling to inadequate
people -- and inadequate people are the main product of
government compulsion schools."
John Taylor Gatto, The Exhausted School: Bending The
Bars Of Traditional Education

"Think of the things killing us as a nation: narcotic
drugs, brainless competition, dishonesty, greed, recre-
ational sex, the pornography of violence, gambling, alcohol, and the worst pornography of all -- lives devoted to buying things, accumulation as a philosophy --
all of these are addictions of dependent personalities.
That is what our brand of schooling must inevitably
produce."

"As society rapidly changes, individuals will have to be able to function comfortably in a world that is always in flux. Knowledge will continue to increase at a dizzying rate. This means that a content-based curriculum, with a set body of information to be imparted to students, is entirely inappropriate as a means of preparing children for their adult roles."

"I've noticed a fascinating phenomenon in my thirty years of teaching: schools and schooling are increasingly irrelevant to the great enterprises of the planet. No one believes anymore that scientists are trained in science classes or politicians in civics classes or poets in English classes. The truth is that schools don't really teach anything except how to obey orders. This is a great mystery to me because thousands of humane, caring people work in schools as teachers and aides and administrators, but the abstract logic of the institution overwhelms their individual contributions. Although teachers to care and do work very, very hard, the institution is psychopathic -- it has no conscience. It rings a bell and the young man in the middle of writing a poem must close his notebook and move to a different cell where he must memorize that humans and monkeys derive from a common ancestor."
John Taylor Gatto, Dumbing Us Down: The Hidden Curriculum of Compulsory Schooling

"Children learn what they live. Put kids in a class and they will live out their lives in an invisible cage, isolated from their chance at community; interrupt kids with bells and horns all the time and they will learn that nothing is important or worth finishing; ridicule them and they will retreat from human association; shame them and they will find a hundred ways to get even. The habits taught in large-scale organizations are deadly."

"Independent study, community service, adventures and experience, large doses of privacy and solitude, a thousand different apprenticeships — the one-day variety or longer — these are all powerful, cheap, and effective ways to start a real reform of schooling. But no large-scale reform is ever going to work to repair our damaged children and our damaged society until we force open the idea of "school" to include family as the main engine of education. If we use schooling to break children away from parents — and make no mistake, that has been the central function of schools since John Cotton announced it as the purpose of the Bay Colony schools in 1650 and Horace Mann announced it as the purpose of Massachusetts schools in 1850 — we're going to continue to have the horror show we have right now."
John Taylor Gatto, Dumbing Us Down: The Hidden Curriculum of Compulsory Schooling

"I've concluded that genius is as common as dirt. We suppress genius because we haven't yet figured out how to manage a population of educated men and women. The solution, I think, is simple and glorious. Let them manage themselves."
John Taylor Gatto, Weapons of Mass Instruction: A Schoolteacher's Journey Through The Dark World of Compulsory Schooling

"This was once a land where every sane person knew how to build a shelter, grow food, and entertain one another. Now we have been rendered permanent children. It's the architects of forced schooling who are responsible for that. School is a twelve-year jail sentence where bad habits are the only curriculum truly learned. I teach school and win awards doing it. I should know."

John Taylor Gatto, Dumbing Us Down: The Hidden Curriculum of Compulsory Schooling

"I don't think we'll get rid of schools any time soon, certainly not in my lifetime, but if we're going to change what's rapidly becoming a disaster of ignorance, we need to realize that the institution "schools" very well, but it does not "educate"; that's inherent in the design of the thing. It's not the fault of bad teachers or too little money spent. It's just impossible for education and schooling to be the same thing."
John Taylor Gatto

"I feel ashamed that so many of us cannot imagine a better way to do things than locking children up all day in cells instead of letting them grow up knowing their families, mingling with the world, assuming real obligations, striving to be independent and self-reliant and free."
John Taylor Gatto

"Pick up a fifth-grade math or rhetoric textbook from 1850 and you'll see that the texts were pitched then on what would today be considered college level. The continuing cry for "basic skills" practice is a smoke screen"

"Work in classrooms isn't significant work; it fails to satisfy real needs pressing on the individual; it doesn't answer real questions experience raises in the young mind; it doesn't contribute to solving any problem encountered in actual life. The net effect of making all schoolwork external to individual longings, experiences, questions, and problems is to render the victim listless."
John Taylor Gatto, The Underground History of American Education: An Intimate Investigation Into the Prison of Modern Schooling

"Mass schooling damages children. We don't need any more of it. And under the guise that it is the same thing as education, it has been picking our pockets just as Socrates predicted it would thousands of years ago. One of the surest ways to recognize real education is by the fact that it doesn't cost very much, doesn't depend on expensive toys or gadgets. The experiences that produce it and the self-awareness that propels it are nearly free. It is hard to turn a dollar on education. But schooling is a wonderful hustle, getting sharper all the time."

"It is time that we squarely face the fact that institutional school teaching is destructive to children."

"What, after all this time, is the purpose of mass schooling supposed to be? Reading, writing, and arithmetic can't be the answer, because properly approached those things take less than a hundred hours to transmit — and we have abundant evidence that each is readily self-taught in the right setting and time. Why, then, are we locking kids up in an involuntary network with strangers for twelve years? Surely not so a few of them can get rich? Even if it worked that way, and I doubt that it does, why wouldn't any sane community look on such an education as positively wrong? It divides and classifies people, demanding that they compulsively compete with each other, and publicly labels the losers by literally degrading them, identifying them as "low-class" material. And the bottom line for the winners is that they can buy more stuff! I don't believe that anyone who thinks about that feels comfortable with such a silly conclusion. I can't help feeling that if we could only answer the question of what it is that we want from these kids we lock up, we would suddenly see where we took a wrong turn. I have enough faith in American imagination and resourcefulness to believe that at that point we'd come up with a better way — in fact, a whole supermarket of better ways."

144

"That seemed crazy on the face of it, but slowly I began to realize that the bells and the confinement, the crazy sequences, the age-segregation, the lack of privacy, the constant surveillance, and all the rest of the national curriculum of schooling were designed exactly as if someone had set out to prevent children from learning how to think and act, to coax them into addiction and dependent behavior."

"We don't need state-certified teachers to make education happen — certification probably guarantees it won't."
John Taylor Gatto, Weapons of Mass Instruction: A Schoolteacher's Journey Through the Dark World of Compulsory Schooling

"People who read too many books get quirky. We can't have too much eccentricity or it would bankrupt us. Market research depends on people behaving as if they were all alike."
John Taylor Gatto, The Underground History of American Education: An Intimate Investigation Into the Prison of Modern Schooling

"The shocking possibility that dumb people don't exist in sufficient numbers to warrant the millions of careers devoted to tending them will seem incredible to you."

"By allowing the imposition of direction from centers far beyond our control, we have time and again missed the lesson of the Congregational principle: people are less than whole unless they gather themselves voluntarily into groups of souls in harmony. Gathering themselves to pursue individual, family, and community dreams consistent with their private humanity is what makes them whole; only slaves are gathered by others. And these dreams must be written locally because to exercise any larger ambition without such a base is to lose touch with the things which give life meaning: self, family, friends, work, and intimate community."

"How many schoolteachers were aware of what they actually were a part of? Surely a number close to zero. In schoolteaching, as in hamburger-flipping, the paycheck is the decisive ingredient. No insult is meant, at bottom this is what realpolitik means. We all have to eat."

And that's the bottom line, people have to eat and school is a business that has made a mess of people. Simple and plain.
More from John Taylor Gatto @ Everything We Think About Schooling Is Wrong! An interview with John Taylor Gotto
https://ttfuture.org/files/2/pdf/gotto_interview.pdf

John Taylor Gatto, rest in peace.

Late to Class: Social Class and Schooling in the New Economy by Jane Van Galen

"Nowhere is there a more intense silence about the realities of class differences than in educational settings." —Bell Hooks

"What does it mean to speak of social class in the United States at the beginning of the twenty-first century? How can formal schooling level playing fields in a rapidly changing economic landscape where the social gap between the "haves" and the "have-nots" is ever widening? It is relatively rare to ask such questions about the relationships between social class and education in the United States, in large measure because Americans have often not known how to think about social class. The deep American faith in education's promise of opportunity represents the contradictions that characterize American beliefs about opportunity and constraint. On the one hand, we believe that school can enable all motivated young people to attain the American dream of self-directed success. On the other hand, we tend to avoid questioning why so many hard-working families have found success elusive in the first place. As we work to prepare students for a new and as-yet unpredictable global economy, it is also time for a renewed interest in how social class shapes the education of young people. Education's promise of opportunity does contain a kernel of truth. For several generations in the twentieth century, most parents performed manual labor to enable their children to aspire to more, and at the same historical moment the economy was creating more white-collar jobs attainable only through educational credentials (Goldin 1998). During this time, many students who did less well in school could still find high-wage jobs in industries and in trades. In today's economy, however, poor and working-class parents are more likely to work multiple low-wage service-sector jobs, and many now find themselves unable to navigate the ever-rising expectations of an increasingly competitive educational system. At a time when many families struggle to balance multiple jobs and parenting, doing well in school is more important than ever: wages have stagnated for those with only a high school education (Day and Newberger 2002), while intense competition among escalating numbers of applicants has transformed the ground rules of college admissions (Golden 2006; Princeton Review n.d.). In this new economy, schools must do much more than promise students that hard work will be rewarded: they must provide the knowledge, support, advocacy, and access that will be needed as more students from marginalized groups aspire to higher educational attainment. In short, educators would be well served by understanding more about how social class shapes educational access, aspiration, and achievement."

"Social class is about not just income (as often suggested in the popular press) but also the degree of
one's personal power and the extent to which one's work
creates dignity and respect (Zweig 2000). According to
Zweig, 62 percent of the workforce is working class,
exercising little control over working conditions or
other workers. Yet beyond hierarchies of income, power,
and status, recent research on class also has also revealed ways in which class is "implicit in everyday social processes and interactions," including classroom
life (Reay 2005, p. 912). Sayer (2005, p. 1) elabo-
rates: Class matters to us not only because of differences in material wealth and economic security, but
also because it affects our access to things, relationships, experiences, and practices which we have reason
to value, and hence our chances of living a fulfill-
ing life. . . . Condescension, deference, shame, guilt,
envy, resentment, arrogance, contempt, fear and mistrust, or simply mutual incomprehension and avoidance
typify relations between people of different classes.
"[C]lass is deeply embedded in everyday interactions,
in institutional processes, in struggles over identity,
validity, self-worth and integrity even when it is not
acknowledged." What may be most insidious, however, is
that within our culture's unquestioning trust in the
power of individuals to make their own way in the American economy, young people are likely to interpret
their parents' and their personal struggles in a shifting economy as evidence of their relative worth and
ability. In the complex process of becoming educated
within social contexts of limited resources, public silence regarding class issues, complex family dynamics,
and peer exclusion, some children come to believe very
early that they deserve relatively little recognition
or status (Jones 2006). Yet aspiring to "more" may be
essential for survival in the new economy. The most
rapid job growth is not among high-tech, high-wage sectors of the economy, but rather among low-wage service

sector jobs, few of which require high levels of education or skill and few of which pay wages sufficient to support a family (Bureau of Labor Statistics 2000). Recent volatility in technology sectors and the stock market, outsourcing, and the rise of contract work have even highly educated workers experiencing an unprecedented sense of economic vulnerability (Ehrenreich 1989, 2005; Berhnhardt et al. 2001; Perucci and Wysong 1999). As Reay (2006, p. 290) has observed, "[C]lass is . . . everywhere and nowhere, denied yet continually enacted."

"The denial of class—and the need to teach more systematically about it—is fueled at least in part by media misrepresentations of social and economic stratification. To many politicians and reporters, the "middle class" includes everyone independent of public assistance or trust funds, even if families vary widely in educational backgrounds, economic security, and personal power. Further, popular representations of poverty and privilege stereotypically conflate race with class (hooks 2000; Jones 2006a; Moss 2003), yet most children in struggling homes in the United States are white. As Kirby Moss has observed, poor whites are rarely mentioned in public discourse about opportunity and the constraints upon it. How then might schools prepare young people for adult lives in such economic and social conditions? Current reform efforts focus almost entirely on raising academic achievement, yet troubling evidence suggests that higher test scores alone won't open opportunities for young people from poor and working-class backgrounds. Even those who succeed in school face uncertainty. Although they have stayed in school longer, the odds of "moving up" to jobs that pay more than one's parents' have declined in the past thirty years (Aaronson and Mazumder 2005). In spite of doing well enough in school to attain good jobs, middle-income families have experienced increasingly sharp declines in household income in the past decade (Hertz 2006). Young people in Canada and many northern European countries have better chances of upward mobility from family origins than do young people in the United States (Hertz 2006). Clearly, the relationships between education and adult success are complex."

"How can young people make sense of the purposes of schooling in volatile economic times? Specifically, how can the children of parents on the margins of the new economy make sense of promises that they can succeed in life through hard work while they watch their hard-working parents struggle? This is clearly a complex challenge. The research collected for Late to Class (Van Galen and Noblit 2007) reveals poor and working-class students tallying the relative costs of loyal identification with their economically vulnerable families against the untested hope that schooling can and will serve their interests. Meanwhile, we also see academically successful, middle-class students come to realize that they have precious little idea of how to navigate the rules of a game that are no longer stable or clear. These contributions show young people living the central questions of class as they negotiate access to school resources, form peer relationships, or try to make sense of the place of schooling in shaping their futures. Yet rarely are they able to name the myriad ways in which social and economic influences shape their lives beyond their own agency. Instead, the research suggests, poor and working-class students most often learn to "settle" for what "people like us" deserve. For example, Julie Bettie (2003, p. 190) observes of girls at the center of these sorts of social confluences: Girls sorted through all of this and began drawing conclusions about what is or is not "for the likes of me and my kind" as friendships were increasingly organized by race/ethnicity and class [and] as girls began to formulate identities based on the possible futures they imagined for themselves."

"Although academic work certainly contributes to how
students can reasonably imagine their possible futures,
the complex social fabric of life in schools and communities also affects those images. As Kaufman (2003)
notes, one cannot merely work one's way into a higher
social status; one's membership must be affirmed by
those already present, and school can provide powerful
indicators about the likelihood of realizing such ambitions. Children coming of age in declining industrial
towns, isolated rural communities, or inner-city areas
encounter daily reminders of the social distance between themselves and their more-privileged peers. Much
more than higher test scores would seem necessary to
invigorate the imagination of such young people. Educators can find it difficult to envision what "more"
might entail, for their imagination can be constrained
by the seeming inevitability of current conditions.
Sayer (2005, p. 1) poignantly argues that class is not
simply a matter of some individuals earning more than
others, but instead encompasses "condescension, deference, shame, guilt, envy, resentment, arrogance, contempt, fear and mistrust." How then might we prepare
young people to cross formidable class boundaries?"

MacKenzie (1998, p. 100) posits that class identity,
unlike race, ethnicity, and gender, is assumed to hold
little academic value. He explains: . . . life for many
poor and working class students is erosively perplexed
by the clinging, deep-rooted suggestion that their
class identity is a badge of cognitive failure, an
identity that an individual of sufficient merit can and
should leave behind—and that one's parents, if clever
and enterprising enough, and unless they're first-gen-
eration immigrants, should have already left behind.
The message is this: Working class students must reme-
diate their identities, and most of them will receive

little or no respect until they do."

"It is difficult to imagine curriculum and pedagogy that enable young people living on the margins of society to embrace both the security their families provide and school norms, in which "success" may imply disparagement of friends and family who are less educated or who work with their hands."
Jane Van Galen, Ph.D., is a professor in the School of Education at the University of Washington, Bothell. With George W. Noblit, she is the co-editor of Late to Class: Social Class and Schooling in the New Economy (State University of New York Press, 2007)

The U.S. Department of Education's spending nationwide is thus: 2016 Actual spending, 14,909,802,000. (Grant total only) 2017 est. 15,459,802,000. (GTO) 2018 est. 14,881,458,000. (GTO)

What are we getting for that? Nothing. The following story is an older report, so we can imagine adjusted for inflation the numbers will be much higher:

America spends more than $600 billion on schools. Here's where it goes and why it matters.
By Libby Nelson@libbyanelson Mar 25, 2015, https://www.vox.com/2015/3/25/8284637/school-spend-ing-US

"By the time a student finishes college, more money is spent on his or her education in America than in nearly every other country in the world. That's because the US, compared with other developed countries, spends a lot on education. Yet all that money is yielding only middling results on international tests. So why is American education so expensive? Partly because other social spending is low; education is expected to play a bigger role in social mobility, particularly for low-income students. And partly because education is mostly a state and local policy issue, so the way the money is spent isn't always equally distributed or particularly logical. School districts in some states spend more to educate wealthy students than poorer ones. The US spends the most per student of any nation in the developed world: $15,171 per student in 2011. The average in the Organization for Economic Co-operation and Development was just $9,313. That number factors in spending by everyone, not just governments. And it includes higher education — which is more expensive in the US than anywhere else in the world. Still, even when you look just at K-12, the US is spending more on each student than most other countries. The US spends $11,193 for each student at the primary levels, more than all but three other nations — Switzerland, Norway, and Luxembourg. Those three, as well as Austria, also spend more than the US on secondary education. The US spends $12,464 per student on high school. But nations that spend less on education are faring far better on international tests, and the US isn't seeing bigger scores as a result of its larger spending. Poland, Finland, and South Korea, where 15-year-olds performed better on those 2012 tests than American students, spend less per student than the US does."

Revenues and Expenditures for Public
Elementary and Secondary Education:
School Year 2014-15 (Fiscal Year 2015)

Selected Findings: Fiscal Year 2015:

"The 50 states and the District of Columbia reported $648.6 billion in revenues collected for public elementary and secondary education in FY 15. State and local governments provided $593.6 billion, or 91.5 per-

cent of all revenues. The federal government contributed $55.0 billion, or 8.5 percent of all revenues
(derived from table 1). Total revenues increased by
3.3 percent (from $628.2 to $648.6 billion) from FY 14
to FY 15, local revenues increased by 3.3 percent
(from $282.5 to $292.0 billion), state revenues increased by 3.7 percent (from $290.7 to $301.6
billion), and federal revenues remained level with an
increase of 0.2 percent (from $54.9 to $55.0 billion)
(derived from tables 1 and 9, after adjusting for inflation).

Total revenues per pupil averaged $12,903 on a national
basis in FY 15 (table 2). This is an increase of 2.7
percent between FY 14 and FY 15, and further builds
upon the increase of 1.2 percent from FY 13 to FY 14
(table 2 after adjusting for inflation). Total revenues
per pupil increased by 3 percent or more in 18 states
and increased by 1 to less than 3 percent in 24 states
from FY 14 to FY 15. Total revenues per pupil decreased
in 4 states between FY 14 to FY 15.

Current expenditures for public elementary and secondary education across the nation increased by 3.3
percent between FY 14 and FY 15 (from $557.5 to $575.8
billion, tables 3 and 9, after adjusting for inflation), following on the heels of an increase of 1.
7 percent from FY 13 to FY 14 (after adjusting for inflation). Expenditures for instruction also increased
by 3.1 percent between FY 14 and FY 15 (from $338.9 to
$349.5 billion). Student support expenditures increased
by 4.5 percent in FY 15 compared to FY 14 (table 9, after adjusting for inflation). Current expenditures per
pupil for public elementary and secondary education
steadily increased between FY 13 to FY 15. Current
expenditures per pupil were $11,454 at the national
level in FY 15, which represents an increase of 2.8
percent from FY 14, following an increase of 1.2 per-

cent from FY 13 (after adjusting for inflation). Current expenditures per pupil ranged from $6,751 in Utah to $20,744 in New York. In addition to New York, current expenditures per pupil were at least 40 percent higher than the national average in the District of Columbia ($20,610), Alaska ($20,191), Connecticut ($19,020), New Jersey ($18,838), Vermont($18,769), Massachusetts ($16,566), and Wyoming ($16,047).Current expenditures per pupil increased by 3 percent or more in 12 states and by 1 to less than 3 percent in 23 states between FY 14 and FY 15 (after adjusting for inflation). Increases in current expenditures per pupil from FY 14 to FY 15 were highest in Alaska (8.6 percent), California (7.3 percent), Texas (4.8 percent), Illinois (4.7 percent), and Maine (4.6 percent).

Current expenditures per pupil decreased by less than 1 percent in 4 states between FY 14 and FY 15. In FY 15, salaries and wages ($328.3 billion) in conjunction with employee benefits ($131.0 billion) accounted for 79.8 percent ($459.3 billion) of current expenditures for public elementary and secondary education. Total expenditures increased by 3.6 percent (from $629.6 to $652.2 billion) between FY 14 and FY 15 (tables 7 and 9, after adjusting for inflation). Of the $652.2 billion in total expenditures, 88.3 percent are current expenditures, 7.8 percent are capital outlay expenditures, 2.7 percent are interest on debt, and 1.3 percent are expenditures for other programs (derived from table 7). States were allocated $14.7 billion in Title I grants for the disadvantaged to spend during the 2014–15 school year.

Title I expenditures (including carryover expenditures) accounted for $14.3 billion, or 2.5 percent of current expenditures for public elementary and secondary education at the national level in FY 15. Title I expenditures per pupil ranged from $140 in Utah to $464 in the

District of Columbia. Title I expenditures per pupil were at least 25 percent higher than the national average in the District of Columbia ($464), Rhode Island ($447), Louisiana ($422), New York ($377), Mississippi ($370), Wyoming ($370), North Carolina ($368), Ohio ($367), Vermont ($365), Montana ($361), and Alaska ($357). Title I expenditures per pupil were at least 25 percent lower than the national average in New Jersey ($209), Idaho ($202), Washington ($201), Connecticut ($194), Virginia ($180), Colorado ($178), Iowa ($175), Minnesota ($172), and Utah ($140)."

Stephen Q. Cornman- National Center for Education Statistics Lei Zhou -Activate Research, Inc.
Malia R. Howell, Jumaane Young- U.S. Census Bureau

That's a lot of money over a generation. In fact, enough to have paid off the mortgages of AMERICANS, and enough to pay people to just stay home from work and read books. Even now, the technology is in place to eliminate physical schools altogether. A laptop and wifi is all that's needed. Online instruction primarily with social activities and support from NGO's, that's it. Slash billions right off the top. Politics, social engineering, values training and all that foolishness that has people nuts needs to be excluded from "education." People are in mental crisis. There has to be change in the way people are educated, for the sake of mental and fiscal health. There is a saying, "pressure will bust a pipe," and its true. The current Prussian "educational" model is having long term psychological damage and financial burden on society. No one had studied this perspective back in 1906-07 when Alexander Inglis wrote his epic Secondary Principles of Education outlining the true nature of "school." available here: https://ia801408.us.archive.org/26/items/principlesof-seco00ingliala/principlesofseco00ingliala.pdf

Nobody knew what 100 years of social engineering would

do to the psyche of a person. Now we know, and we keep throwing money at a losing proposition. What difference does it make of how many people have college degrees when people are sleeping in the streets of the wealthiest nation on earth? Who gives a shit? Who cares about the next award show or celebrity sighting when some bum is pissing in an open air urinal in San Francisco:

"A lawsuit filed by a religious group seeking the removal of an open-air urinal or "pissoir" recently installed at Dolores Park has been dismissed by a San Francisco Superior Court judge. The decision, filed Sept. 30 by Judge Harold Kahn, dismisses the lawsuit filed in April on behalf of the San Francisco Chinese Christian Union by the Pacific Justice Institute, a conservative nonprofit. "The installation and maintenance of the pissoir does not contravene any of the constitutional provisions, statutes or common law rules cited by plaintiffs nor, even if it did, would there be any basis to issue the requested injunctive relief," Kahn wrote. The lawsuit alleged the urinal, located near a J-Church light-rail stop on the edge of the park, violates laws regarding privacy, sex discrimination, public health, access for persons with a disability and the plumbing code. The pissoir was installed in response to neighborhood complaints about public urination by park goers in the area."?

By Sara Gaiser Bay City News 10/10/2016 https://www.n-bcbayarea.com/news/local/Chinese-Christian-Group-Neighbors-Sue-Over-Pissor-Public-Urinal-in-San-Francisco-Alleges--376217531.html

Who cares when grandma cant go shopping for food without worrying about how she's gonna pay for it, or if somebody is gonna knock her in the head and take it? The revenue waste of the current model is a no brainer from a business perspective because its good money after bad. We spend billions up front (school) to produce a product that costs billions on the back end to maintain (broken people). The amount of money spent does not make the few people who do succeed a value. Something is wrong with that picture and people have to scrutnize this spending behavior and make an honest determination if it makes sense relative to expenditures. Again, we cant keep breaking children and the bank and expect to win. In New York for example:

"DHS's 2017 budget totals a record $1.7 billion, 20 percent more than the $1.4 billion the agency spent in 2016. The agency's budget is $172 million ($100 million in city funds) greater than the budget presented in the November 2016 Financial Plan. The budget for shelter capacity, which includes intake, administration and operation of family and adult shelters, is now $1.4 billion. BO estimates that, given current trends in the shelter population and shelter pricing, an additional $190 million ($165 million in city funds) will be needed to adequately cover shelter expenses over the course of 2018, with the majority of the new funds needed for single adult shelters. These additional funds would increase the 2018 budget for shelter costs to $1.4 billion, compared with the $1.2 billion the city currently has budgeted....continued increases in the cost of sheltering the city's homeless population is likely to be the norm over the next few years."
Prepared by Sarah Stefanski New York City Independent Budget Office February 2017- "Homeless Shelter Costs Continue to Be Underbudgeted in Future Years"

That's just one city alone, so imagine the entire nation's budget spent on homelessness. School is not preparing the populace for success....obviously. The mere fact of this is an open proof:

WHAT IT WOULD COST TO SHELTER EVERY PERSON ON L.A.'S STREETS?

"$657 million. That's according to a new report from the L.A. Homeless Services Authority. That's the first year. After that, the report found that it would cost the city about $354 million a year to run the shelter system. That's not a high estimate. New York City, which runs a shelter system for all but a few thousand of its 77,000 homeless people, spends well over $2 billion a year on shelters."

by Rina Palta in News on June 22, 2018

https://laist.com/2018/06/22/heres_what_it_would_cost_to_shelter.php

The aforementioned figures are yearly, every year in the foreseeable future in just two cities. The populace is not being prepared for success, as is evident.

"Some underlying assumptions. Social theory must always furnish the basis whereon are established conceptions of the functions which education should perform. The social theory underlying the considerations adduced in this chapter involves certain assumptions the substantiation of which cannot be attempted here. Among those assumptions the more fundamental are the following:
(1) Society is to be conceived as in evolutionary process. In that process are involved the two factors of integration and differentiation, the former working toward social cohesion and solidarity, the latter working toward variation and modification.
(2) There is an essential congruity of interest between the individual and society. The possibility of the development of the individual is found in his participation in social activities and in the social consciousness. The possibility of the development of society is found in the development of social personalities in individuals.

(3) The school is to be considered as a social institution or agency maintained by society for the purpose of assisting in then maintenance of its own stability and in the direction of its own progress. If the school is to be looked on as an institution established, maintained, and controlled by society for the purpose of maintaining its own stability and determining the direction of its own progress, secondary education, as a part (and as apart only) of a general system of education, must be conceived as determined fundamentally by its functions as a social agency. Looked at from this point of view secondary education involves a number of important social principles some of which may be formulated here and considered further in following sections.

(1) The character and purposes of secondary education at any time and in any society must conform to the dominant ideals and to the form of social organization of that society.
(2) The dynamic character of the social process requires the constant readjustment of secondary education to the changing demands of society.
(3) The nature of social evolution involves the two supplementary factors of integration and differentiation, both of which must be recognized properly in secondary education.
(4) Whenever any other social institution fails to provide forms of education socially desirable the school should assume responsibility for those forms of education as far as may be possible. Whenever such forms of education are appropriate to the age and grade of secondary education, the secondary school should assume responsibility for them. Conversely, whenever other social agencies provide adequately for forms of education socially desirable the school should not attempt to assume responsibility for them. In discussing the historical development of secondary education the point was

emphasized that the efficiency of the secondary school is to be measured in terms of the degree in which it conforms and contributes to the dominant social ideals and form of social organization at any particular time. In discussing systems of secondary education in different countries the point was emphasized that the efficiency of the secondary PRINCIPLES OF SECONDARY EDUCATION school is to be measured according to the dominant social ideals and the form of social organization peculiar to each country. In the present section the principles of education involved may be considered with special reference to the social ideals and social organization of the American Democracy. To state that the American secondary school should conform to the democratic ideals and the democratic organization of American society is to state a platitude. The implications of such a statement, however, are not always clearly perceived and may bear further consideration. Three important implications invite attention.

(1) Efficient membership in American society demands at least three qualifications:

(a) an ability effectively to execute the formal and informal duties of citizenship and carry the burden of political responsibility;

(b) an ability to produce and labor sufficiently to carry one's own economic load;

(c) an ability to utilize one's leisure time and act in an individual capacity without interfering with the interests of others or of society at large. In certain societies where other social ideals are dominant it is possible for many of the privileges and responsibilities of citizenship to be prerogatives of special groups. In some forms of society it is possible for economic production to rest principally on certain groups. In certain forms of society opportunities for the enjoyment of leisure are open to different groups in degrees determined by social ideals which greatly limit certain individuals or groups. In the American democracy the three forms of activity must be considered as important for every citizen in so far as his individual capacity and circumstances permit. It follows, therefore, not only that educational opportunity, including secondary education, should be universal in America, but also that these three phases of activity must be conceived as necessary parts of the education due every individual and that in the secondary school each of the three phases should receive attention in due proportion. Failure to recognize this principle in the past has led to over emphasis on certain phases of secondary]education and the comparative neglect of others. This is particularly noticeable in the comparative neglect until recently of the preparation of the worker in the American secondary school. Over-emphasis in the other direction for some pupils is a not impossible tendency in some quarters at the present time.

(2) It must be recognized that in American society each individual must be not merely a law-abiding citizen but also to some extent a law-making citizen. It must further be recognized that the minimum level of general intelligence necessary in any society must depend on the amount of privilege conferred on the individual and the amount of responsibility placed on him. In a society where for the majority of individuals the great necessity is conformance to imposed demands, a much lower level of general intelligence is required than in a society where the individual must not only conform to social demands but also determine in part what those demands shall be. Further, it must be recognized that with the constantly growing complexity of modern social and economic life the amount of intelligence and training necessary to meet its privileges and responsibilities is much greater than at any former time. An education which was adequate for the needs of a simpler social organization cannot be adequate for the needs of a more complex society. Consequently it has becomes a serious problem in this country whether steps should not

be taken to provide that a larger proportion of
prospective members of American society should
receive the benefits of education beyond theelementary
school.

The increased privileges and responsibilities granted
to and demanded of the individual in American society
cannot be provided for by a system which gives two
thirds of the citizens not more than an elementary education. The complicated social problems of modern civic
and industrial life and of individual conduct cannot be
understood and intelligently attacked by a people two
thirds of whom have received elementary instruction
only and of which on the average individuals have received much less than one thousand days of schooling
each. Unless the average amount of education received
can be markedly increased the further development
of American democracy must be seriously conditioned if
not actually imperiled. The problem is one affecting
most secondary education in the public schools.
(3) The participation of all citizens in the direction
and control of all social institutions of a public nature includes a participation in the direction and control of the school as well as of other institutions.
The agency on which democracy must most depend is one
which democracy must itself determine and control. Even
more than in most societies the American secondary
school must conform to social ideals and the form of
social organization."
Alexander Inglis, Secondary principles of education pp.
340-343. 1907

This book lays the entire plan out, its actually quite
mater of fact. One cannot fully understand this topic
without reading this book and it more relevant than
ever, specifically since we all now see what the level
of substandard education has done to the currently re-
volting, Covid-19, brainwashed population.

CONCLUSION

In the 1976 movie "Network" there is a scene, and in
this particlar scene a speech is given to a news re-
porter. That same speech is revelant today and should
be firmly understood in the context of this book. This
is the speech that should be given to the schools. The
parts of history covered,the creation of this "nation,"
the bloody past and all of the events attached thereto,
are all part of ideals well beyond any foolishness being spewed upon the children. If children were perhaps
taught the real way the game goes, then maybe, just
maybe those children will grow up and be about the peoples business in a meaningful way. The speech is as
follows:

"Arthur Jensen: You have meddled with the primal forces
of nature, Mr. Beale, and I won't have it! Is that
clear? You think you've merely stopped a business deal.
That is not the case! The Arabs have taken billions of
dollars out of this country, and now they must put it
back! It is ebb and flow, tidal gravity! It is ecologi-
cal balance! You are an old man who thinks in terms of
nations and peoples. There are no nations. There are no
peoples. There are no Russians. There are no Arabs.
There are no third worlds. There is no West. There is
only one holistic system of systems, one vast and im-
mane, interwoven, interacting, multivariate, multina-
tional dominion of dollars. Petro-dollars, electro-dol-
lars, multi-dollars, reichmarks, rins, rubles, pounds,
and shekels. It is the international system of currency
which determines the totality of life on this planet.
That is the natural order of things today. That is the
atomic and subatomic and galactic structure of things
today! And YOU have meddled with the primal forces of
nature, and YOU, WILL, ATONE! Am I getting through to
you, Mr. Beale? You get up on your little twenty-one
inch screen and howl about America and democracy. There

is no America. There is no democracy. There is only
IBM, and ITT, and AT&T, and DuPont, Dow, Union Carbide,
and Exxon.[Editor's note: Microsoft, Google, Youtube,
Amazon, Twitter] Those are the nations of the world today. What do you think the Russians talk about in their
councils of state, Karl Marx? They get out their linear
programming charts, statistical decision theories, min-
imax solutions, and compute the price-cost probabili-
ties of their transactions and investments, just like
we do. We no longer live in a world of nations and ide-
ologies, Mr. Beale. The world is a college of corpora-
tions, inexorably determined by the immutable bylaws of
business. The world is a business, Mr. Beale. It has
been since man crawled out of the slime. And our children will live, Mr. Beale, to see that... perfect
world... in which there's no war or famine, oppression
or brutality. One vast and ecumenical holding company,
for whom all men will work to serve a common profit, in
which all men will hold a share of stock. All necessi-
ties provided, all anxieties tranquilized, all boredom
amused. And I have chosen you, Mr. Beale, to preach
this evangel."
The film " Network," (1976) clip @ https://www.y-
outube.com/watch?v=yuBe93FMiJc
https://www.americanrhetoric.com/MovieSpeeches/moviespe
echnetwork4.html

Get it? Instead of raising a nation of grown up problem
children, how about raising a nation of businessmen and
women? Instead of throwing billions at a useless
school, how about turning those secondary schools into
vocational centers where each teen graduates with a vocation? Each school should be mandated to have two or
more vocational programs. Welding, Auto Mechanics,
Writing Code, Stone Masons, Medical/Dental, Carpentry,
Sheet Metal Fabricating, business management etc., with
a two year certification. Each secondary school should
be required to graduate each senior class student with

a certification for a specific vocation or no 500 billion. That will insure a constant pool of "skilled"
laborers that are wage earners, home owners, tax pay-
ers, generating tangible revenue, and most importantly,
making shit! Manufacturing goods at home. This is
doable in 4 years. Two years to set it up and two years
to graduate the first mass national batch of skilled
workers. That would have a profound effect upon the national GDP and its would start the process of eliminat-
ing homelessness, and the generational poverty of most
all Americans. Right now we are just mass producing
mentally ill debt slaves, and burden. A child is forced
into a school program that generationally, at least for
the poor, has mass produced nothing but homelessness,
prison fodder, more poverty, drug use, alcoholism, un-
employment, welfare dependency, low morals, crime, sexual deviancy and rebellion against the progression of
the species....This has been going on for generations
and people somehow still believe that this school model
is helping. The current model may help 1 in 250 on a
good day, so the other 249 are fodder for all of the
aforementioned adversities. There "must" be a "school
structure," indeed, however there must be a serious
reevaluation of the current model, by an independent
arbiter, as to whether or not fiscally the current model has in the past maximized the potential of the people or funding, and most importantly, whether the current model can fulfill the potential that is needed to
adequately compete in the future world of global economics. Graduating a million people with degrees who
don't know what a pipe a wrench looks like is crippling
the GDP of the whole and only rewarding "that" segment,
meanwhile billions of dollars in human potential lay
dormant, watching comic book mega movies and pornography. Marinating in street drugs, doctor drugs, alcohol,
silly filthy rap music, weed, inter alia, social media,
fake social justice causes,and all manners of perver-
sion, all legal, all normal, while a thousand scien-

tists, mathematicians, quantum physicists, intellectual potential, skilled labor, tax revenue, related business activity, and their revenue streams, billions, gets wiped....yearly, for generations (Toilet flushing in the background)! Fortnite anyone? Or maybe Black Panther? When one couples the school fiasco with the racial components that are constantly propagated, is it any wonder why people are so broken? The White folk have been strutting around thinking its all good, and everyone else is a nigger, when in reality they're niggers too. They started off genetically as niggers, came to America, and became "a nigger at once" if they crossed the wrong path. The Whites would get the 'ole dip 'n dye, and off to the auction block. Niggers owned plenty white folk and White folk owned plenty niggers. There must have been a lot of whites owned, because anytime a law is passed making it illegal for niggers to do something it has to have been a lot niggers doing it. If Black people owned white slaves it would be naive to think they were not being treated in like manner as the black slaves. The white slaves were working, serving, getting their asses kicked, and getting pregnant just like the black slaves. Those children are running around all over America right now in different skin. Transplanted organs functions in black and white and so does that sperm and egg. The point being that it is time to get past the old racial past, it's crippling the populace. Black men fought for the Confederacy, hell, we fought everybody, EVERYWHERE, for this, our native land too, and that cant be "white washed" by silly pseudo scholars. I know it breaks the brain of some whites to know they were chattel slaves, and I know some black people will view themselves differently. For my White brothers and sisters I would like you to hear it from your own, because most brainwashed people dont believe shit unless some White man is telling it to them...

> # THE IRISH ARE THE NIGGERS OF EUROPE, LADS. AN' DUBLINERS ARE THE NIGGERS OF IRELAND.... AN' THE NORTHSIDE DUBLINERS ARE THE NIGGERS O' DUBLIN. - SAY IT LOUD, I'M BLACK AN' I'M PROUD.
>
> - RODDY DOYLE -

Now I know I am going to catch a lot of heat from the brainwashed Negros who will claim, "He's an apologist for Whites." I realize there will be nigga's coming out in Dashiki's 'n beads 'n shit growling about the content of my work and how I'm this or that, and I'm cool with that, cuz I don't give shit. I don't apologize for the racist devil, who usurps the Confederate flag and utilizes it as a tool for terror and intimidation. Or on the same token, I don't shield the fanatic who wants to tear down that flag or monuments. (Which is happening now in 2020, this book was written in 2018-19) I don't shield or condone any acts upon anyone historically that have resulted in the shed of the blood of innocents. I don't now, nor will I ever validate many of policies that I see the organized corporate construct implement, however, how much lamentation? A hundred years, a thousand? How much past baggage do we continually carry as a people? When do Americans give themselves permission to move on. When do Americans finally say to themselves, "Yes, we have done some horrible, evil, dirty, low down shit to get to this point we are at in this society, WTF!?" Nobody's hands are clean, and nobody has the life they have now, living in America, save it for the blood, treasure and souls shed to get here. That's fact. Has not the time come for people to realize their true places in this saga, acknowledge its tragedy, and atone for it in a meaningful way by altering behaviors and attitudes now and in the future? Has not the time come for people to know their past, know the mistakes, and know the successes in order to navigate into a prosperous future? Racism-classism is a start, and for all of the die hard people of "pure" racial pedigree....reality check, you're niggers too. If you received a vaccination in the last 40 50 years then guess what:

Honoring Henrietta:
The Legacy of
Henrietta Lacks

In 1951, a young mother of five named Henrietta Lacks visited The Johns Hopkins Hospital complaining of vaginal bleeding. Upon examination, renowned gynecologist Dr. Howard Jones discovered a large, malignant tumor on her cervix. At the time, The Johns Hopkins Hospital was one of only a few hospitals to treat poor African-Americans. As medical records show, Mrs. Lacks began undergoing radium treatments for her cervical cancer. This was the best medical treatment available at the time for this terrible disease. A sample of her cancer cells retrieved during a biopsy were sent to Dr. George Gey's nearby tissue lab. For years, Dr. Gey, a prominent cancer and virus researcher, had been collecting cells from all patients who came to The Johns Hopkins Hospital with cervical cancer, but each sample quickly died in Dr. Gey's lab. What he would soon discover was that Mrs. Lacks' cells were unlike any of the others he had ever seen: where other cells would die, Mrs. Lacks' cells doubled every 20 to 24 hours. Today, these incredible cells— nicknamed "HeLa" cells, from the first two letters of her first and last names — are used to study the effects of toxins, drugs, hormones and viruses on the growth of cancer cells without experimenting on humans. They have been used to test the effects of radiation and poisons, to study the human genome, to learn more about how viruses work, and played a crucial role in the development of the polio vaccine. Although Mrs. Lacks ultimately passed away on October 4, 1951, at the age of 31, her cells continue to impact the world. https://www.hopkinsmedicine.org/henriettalacks/

Oops, the social controllers forgot to tell you that, your are definitely niggers too.

Lastly, it was shown, the very complex business dynamic involved in the creation of the United States project. Just as today, there are international players, Muslim nations, who play a significant role in the success or failure of financial projects worldwide. The Judas goat media is constantly "Nat. Turnering" Muslim people and fostering another revenue stream loss (Islamic wealth). There would be no America as we know it without those international players, Muslim and non-Muslim alike. The entire "white patriot" founding fathers movement somehow leaves out these facts. We are all Americans, some

of us aboriginal, most of us mutts, and we all have a
stake in the outcome of this project. We have to get
back to a place where people talk to each other, and
people take pride in their dress, homes and their
lives. We have to try something new because the same
'ole same 'ole just ain't working. My apologies to anyone whom I have offended, as with anything, one size
does not fit all, and there are teachers, educators and
academics trying really hard. To you I mean no offense.
I additionally mean no offense in my usage of "nigger."
I use it for shock value, and because people need to
hear it spoken and know it is a hurtful descriptive
term encompassing behavior, appearance, and social status. Besides a lot of people, of all races, act like
niggers. We've all been niggers once, and if we are not
careful, we will be all niggers again. If we let the
silly rappers have their way, we will always be niggers. If we let the schools "educate" us in the current
model, we will always be niggers, if we keep idolizing
celebrities who do nothing for us, we will always be
niggers. If we stay in the same mentality, we will always be niggers and if we don't change our hearts it
wont matter. It boggles my mind to watch a person buy
20 dollars worth of dog food while holding a little
dog, walk out of the store right past a person sleeping
on the streets and not even give them a quarter. Or the
thousands of lonely women, longing for someone to love
them, someone to need them, so they buy a dog while
thousands of children rot in foster care. Or the cow-
ardly churches that own millions of acres of land nationwide, that sits EMPTY every night, while a mother
and her children sleep in a car on the street, and they
church leaders buy 50 million dollar Jets and 200,000
cars for their wives (Hypocrites). Or the veteran, who
put it "all" on the line, for the ideals of this nation, slow dying, one cell at a time, in plain view,
while the world goes on oblivious to their suffering.
Or the child, brainwashed from day one, who could have

created something to change the world, instead they created nothing, and died inside over a lifetime, one slight after another, for nothing.......... How long until the "progressive," harmonious world we profess we want materializes? I suspect never. Because we talk a good national game 'o shit, and we have made an art out of illusion, theater, grandstanding, and sounding authoritative, however after all these generations of devolving, that shit is tired. Only the silly, naive people still bite. Its only so much fronting one can do, eventually people catch on. Hopefully this work will start a conversation that leads to something tangible for one person at least. If one person shows another some love, picks up a book, is kind to a stranger ...I'm good. My people used to tell me, "God sits High and He looks low." Well if that is true, I want my record to reflect, I tried. I tried for the children when others silently capitulated, subconsciously resigned to narrow hearts, became spectator's to their own demise, and loved every minute of it... damn!

I would like to thank all of the authors and writers whose work I compiled to make my point, without you none of this would be possible, and I would like to thank my family,children and grands, and of course, The Queen Bee, my beloved.

A special thanks to D.L. Hugley, who explained in one sentence a millennium of what can be described as, mental illness and reactionary violence. To elaborate: The fear created through the media about the "persona" of the "Black" man in America, has made the White man scared and prone to violence towards Black men from that fear. Sad part most of that created fear is just a figment of whites own imagination and a push from the media of course, all for profit and control. If you were to take 10 White people, give them a drawing pad and ask them to draw a "Scary Nigger," each would have

172

a different drawing based upon their own IMAGINATION. The more frightened the person, the scarier the imagined "nigger," and the more dangerous the scared person becomes towards the "nigger." That's a dangerous place to exist in.

A woodcut (based on a photograph) that was published in *Harper's Weekly* on 30 January 1864 with the caption, "EMANCIPATED SLAVES, WHITE AND COLORED."

Jean-Baptiste Guillory (1766-1813) is the 4th Great Grandfather of this author. He is a veteran of the American Revolution, Battle of Baton Rouge (1790), representing the Attakapas Militia, a slave owner and "Free Person of Color" listed in the 1790 Opelousas Census, as Mulatto (French and Attakapas) and Free.

2020 ENDNOTE

When this book was first written in 2018-19, I had no idea just how relevant it would become. I had no idea that the nation would be in upheaval, and I had no idea that Black Lives Matter would become a defining entity in that upheaval.

Racial injustice, racial strife, police brutality have become part and parcel with daily life in the United States and the fruits of such has become manifest. The populace has become even more galvanized upon racial lines and the possibility of civil war is greater than ever.

It is this author's hopes that racial division will vanish and that the citizens of this nation will realize that they are all being led down a path to destruction by the same forces who once led a previous rebellion. The result will be the same. There is no division, except the division created by the media and politicians who care not for the people, but only for their own power. May THE MOST HIGH guide, protect and heal this nation and its misguided, grieving populace.

Printed in Great Britain
by Amazon

51879207R00104